"Everything is described so clearly...a joy to read...I got so excited that as soon as I finished reading *Travel Free!*, I rushed to the phone, called my retired mother and my daughter at college, and told them about the book...I'm seriously contemplating starting my own Travel Consultant business!"

— Sharon Scholtz,
Fashion Model and Single Parent

"Through their travel industry experience and insight and their unique ability to express it, Ben and Nancy Dominitz have put together the first significant text for outside Travel Consultants. This book will be of *tremendous* benefit to those working in outside sales, to those contemplating doing so, and to all other travel agents—whether they be owners, managers, or inside agents—who need to understand better our industry's rapidly growing outside sales force."

— William E. Stephan,
President of M.I.T.A.
(Membership of Individual Travel Agents)

"Typesetting *Travel Free!* has created pandemonium in our office. After reading the book, our entire staff is eager to become Travel Consultants, and I am sorely tempted to join them!"

— Tom DeLapp, Owner of
Pacific Communications Group

"*Travel Free!* provides essential information and incentives to anyone interested in the rewards of travel. In addition, it offers fresh insight and sales techniques to those already in the travel industry."

— Will Noble, C.T.C.,
Travel Writer, and Consultant

"Dominitz has contributed experienced insight and creative ideas that should motivate and assist many who aspire to travel while actually making money."

— Baxter and Corinne Geeting,
Authors of *Confessions of a Tour Leader*

TRAVEL FREE
**How to Start and Succeed in
Your Own Travel Consultant Business**

TRAVEL FREE
How to Start and Succeed in Your Own Travel Consultant Business

Ben Dominitz
with
Nancy D. Dominitz

Prima
Publishing and Communications
Carmichael, California

Quantity discounts are available from:

Prima Publishing and Communications
Post Office Box 1550
Carmichael, CA 95608
Telephone: (916) 972-8777

Library of Congress Cataloging in Publication Data
Dominitz, Ben, 1950-
Travel free.

"Travel trade publications in the United States and Canada" p.
Includes index.
1. Travel agents—Vocational guidance. I. Dominitz, Nancy D. II. Title.
G154.66 1984   380.1'459104'068   83-63113
ISBN 0-914629-00-X

Book design and typesetting:
Pacific Communications Group, Sacramento, California

Printed in U.S. by:
R.R. Donnelley & Sons Company in Crawfordsville, Indiana

*To all our friends and adversaries
from whom we have learned so much.*

TABLE OF CONTENTS

PREFACE AND ACKNOWLEDGMENTS

This is the first of several books which we intend to write together. In this case, the book was primarily written by Ben, who is the business expert of our team. Since it is our habit to work on projects together, many of the ideas, recommendations, and stylistic touches were the inspiration of Nancy. For smoother reading, however, the first person singular is used throughout the text.

As is the case with most writers, gender usage presented a challenge. When first preparing the text, and in the custom of our day, we interchanged the pronouns, "he/him" with "she/her," at random. However, upon reading the results, which we found to be awkward and artificial, we resorted to the standard usage of employing the pronouns, "he/him," to include "she/her."

For the use of their materials in this book, we would like to thank and acknowledge the following:

● Alexander Anolik, Attorney at Law, for the inclusion of the materials from *Preventive Legal Care.*

● Jeanne Gay for the inclusion of her customer survey.

● Baxter and Corinne Geeting for permission to use an excerpt from *Confessions of a Tour Leader.*

● The Institute of Certified Travel Agents for the inclusion of an excerpt from *Systematic Management of Outside Sales,* a thesis researched and written by Janet Farro, C.T.C., as an academic requirement for certification in the Executive Travel Management Program of the Institute; Copyright 1982.

● *TravelAge West,* an OAG publication, for the use of various excerpts.

● *Webster's New World Dictionary, Second College Edition,* Copyright 1982 by Simon and Schuster, Inc., for permission to use their definition for the entry, "transportation."

● Ziff-Davis Publishing Co. for the inclusion of the *ABC's of Travel* from *Travel Weekly* magazine.

In addition, our thanks to the following people:

● For editorial help, Will Noble, C.T.C.; Baxter and Corinne Geeting; and Alexander Anolik.

● For dedication and professionalism, the staff at Pacific Communications Group and R.R. Donnelley & Sons Company.

Finally, special thanks go to Nancy Martinelli, our exceptional assistant and friend, who "held down the fort" while we were immersed with this project.

Ben and Nancy Dominitz
Carmichael, California
December, 1983

When I was very young and the urge to be someplace else was on me, I was assured by mature people that maturity would cure this itch. When years described me as mature, the remedy prescribed was middle age. In middle age I was assured that greater age would calm my fever, and now that I am fifty-eight perhaps senility will do the job.
JOHN STEINBECK

CHAPTER ONE

THE BEST-KEPT SECRET...

WHAT THIS BOOK WILL DO FOR YOU

There are many ways you can benefit from this book. You will learn how you can, **right now**, become a member of the glamorous travel industry. You will be able to start part time or full time, without an investment, out of your own home. As a Travel Consultant, you will be able to generate a new source of income to do with as you wish—and these days, who couldn't use more money in his pockets? In addition, as a respected member of the travel industry, you will learn about fabulous travel opportunities at great discounts and enjoy other exclusive benefits. No more wishful thinking for you about that vacation in Hawaii! No more "flea bag" motels in your future! From now on, you can earn the right to travel in luxury and often at a mere fraction of normal costs.

In this book, I will share with you the "ins and outs" of succeeding in the travel business. Even if you have no previous experience in travel, the "good life" can be yours if you are a person with drive and personal initiative. You may be a corporate or government employee seeking a window of opportunity in which to escape boredom and make more money. You may be an older citizen looking for an exciting new way to supplement your retirement income. Perhaps you are a woman with children who wants to start a rewarding career without having to get an outside job. Even if you are already the owner of your own business, you may be eager to diversify your income while offsetting your travel expenses. Or, are you an enterprising student who is willing to work hard to qualify for free travel and make extra money? Whoever you are—young or elderly, over-educated or street-wise, a world-weary traveler or a neophyte—you can benefit from becoming a Travel Consultant.

Sound unbelievable? It isn't. Since 1977, Nancy and I have arranged group trips as Travel Consultants. During this time, we have crisscrossed the United States several times, relaxed on the beaches of the Caribbean, lain on the pink sands of Bermuda, and returned to Hawaii's lushness again and again. We have stayed in some of the world's most luxurious hotels and resorts, often in V.I.P. suites. All this and more, we have done for nominal costs and sometimes at no cost at all. Make no mistake about it, we have earned these privileges, but it has been pleasant and always fascinating work.

In addition to our own practical experience, we have spared no effort in collecting the best available information on the subject of how to start and succeed in your own Travel Consultant business. We have scoured the trade publications, attended seminars, and studied graduate theses written for the Institute of Certified Travel Agents. We have also interviewed various members of the travel industry. It would have taken anyone many months and hundreds, even thousands, of dollars to compile this information on his own. This treasure of knowledge is now available to you for the modest cost of this book.

TRAVEL CONSULTANT—A DEFINITION

What is a Travel Consultant, anyway? What does one have to do to participate in this unique package of income and travel benefits? If you are new to the travel industry, these are, no doubt, some of the questions you're now entertaining. As the name implies, a Travel Consultant is a woman or man who consults with the public on their travel needs. Unlike travel agents, who normally wait for someone to call or drop by in order to make a sale, Travel Consultants bring their business to their clients' home or office. In order to become a member of the industry, Travel Consultants need to affiliate themselves with a travel agency. Although they work with a travel agency, Travel Consultants act as independent contractors, which makes them self-employed. As a Travel Consultant, you can choose to work on a part-time or full-time basis—it's up to you. You will be paid by receiving a percentage of the commission or earnings received by the travel agency for the business you produce. In addition to the opportunity to earn substantial income, you, as a Travel Consultant, will qualify for various travel and educational benefits which are available exclusively to members of the retail travel "family." Chapters three and four are devoted to a complete explanation of the incomes and travel benefits which you can enjoy.

The term, "Travel Consultant," is a relatively new one. Until now, "outside sales" has been the standard industry expression attached to those who sell travel "outside" the agency's premises. It evolved from a need to differentiate between the "outside sales" staff, who are self-employed, and the "inside sales" or agency-bound employees. This book, however, makes an attempt to steer away from the "outside sales" terminology whenever possible. Why? According to a recent survey among travel agency owners, most felt that the "inside" and "outside" terms created a barrier between the two groups. In addition, the title, "outside sales," has no meaning to the public. In fact, it sounds downright objectionable. Still not sure which terminology you prefer? Try this experiment. Imagine that you are at a cocktail party. A delightful member of the opposite sex engages you in casual conversation. At the appropriate moment, usually after, "And where are you from?", the inevitable question, "And what do you do?" pops up. Picture yourself answering, "I'm in outside sales." Now try, "I'm a Travel Consultant." Need I state the obvious? Case closed.

WHY THIS BOOK WAS WRITTEN

This book was written for the best possible reason. To my knowledge, no major publication has ever appeared on the rapidly growing field of outside sales in travel. The thought of completing the first book on this emerging profession has infused this project with an air of adventure. After all, if you want to learn how to operate a mail-order business, you can choose from hundreds of books and articles which examine every aspect from A to Z. Even the subject of how to publish your own book is represented by a growing stack of printed matter—much of it self-published. But here is a major career, a profession providing employment to thousands of men and women throughout North America; and yet, very few people outside the travel industry are aware of its existence.

Why is this so? Why has this profession largely escaped the notice of the majority of opportunity seekers? One of the reasons is that outside travel sales is a relatively new career. Although we know of people who have been selling travel services by visiting commercial establishments as early as twenty-five years ago, this field is emerging only now as a vital force within the travel industry. Until recently, the majority of travel agencies did not feel the need to expand their marketing programs. They were riding the crest of a wave of unprecedented growth. This growth was so extensive that from 1960 to 1980, passenger air travel increased by almost 500%. In addition, an important policy change by the airlines was extremely useful in diverting more business to the travel agencies. In the early 1960s, the airlines handled most of the sales of tickets to the public directly. But as their costs of ticketing and making reservations climbed to 15% of their operating expenses, the airlines started to promote the travel agencies through their advertising. "Call Your Travel Agent" became a familiar slogan. During this "golden period," travel agents began to expect an ever-growing clientele. Also, a few years ago, agency incomes received a "shot in the arm" when the airlines began to pay travel agents a 10% commission instead of 7% on most ticket sales. As a result of all these factors, many agents became lax in the marketing of their services. "After all," they thought, "we don't really have to go out and sell—our clients will come to us."

By 1980, this honeymoon period of easy growth was over. The recessionary-inflationary cycle forced individuals and corporations to become more prudent in their use of air travel. Today, to survive and to succeed, both the airlines and the travel agencies must develop strong marketing programs. There is a growing concensus that they must aggressively sell their services to new customers and instill greater loyalty in their established clients. The need to compete effectively in today's marketplace explains the emergence of the Travel Consultant. Instead of sitting at the office, waiting for a client to call or drop in, the Travel Consultant visits his clients on their own "turf." By bringing his service to the customer, he can create new business that otherwise would have been lost.

Another reason why the field of outside sales has existed in relative obscurity can be explained by the closed-circuit, inbred attitudes still prevalent in some segments of the travel community. There are a few in the industry who do not want the rest of the world to discover the great opportunities available within the travel trade. These threatened individuals suffer from an attitude of "lack." People with this mentality believe that there is only so much business to be had. Therefore, any new person who enters into the travel business, they fear, will split a finite pie into smaller slices. The industry, in its entirety, stands to lose much from this parochial attitude. Why? Because many who have never before traveled on a commercial carrier will now become enthusiastic first-time travelers through the pleasant persistence of a Travel Consultant. Like any other business, the travel trade needs the infusion of new talent and vision in order to stimulate new growth. Among the readers of this book, there will be many who may have had no previous background in travel but who are highly motivated to succeed. They will bring their creativity and energy to the industry. As a result, everyone will benefit. The world of travel will be enriched with more individual and group business, travel agencies will generate new accounts, and exciting, lucrative new careers will be launched.

IT'S UP TO YOU

The opportunities in outside sales are enormous. As you study the contents of this book, you will realize that the amount of income you can generate is controlled only by your actions and creativity. You may choose, as others have done, to build a profitable, full-time business as a Travel Consultant; or, you may decide that a part-time venture suits your needs best.

There is a fable told about the three travelers who stumbled upon a gold mine in the desert. The first traveler, in his excitement, stuffed his pockets with as much gold as they could hold and continued on his journey, a little richer and a little heavier. The second traveler, a bit wiser, emptied his satchel and filled it *and* his pockets with all the gold he could carry. The third traveler, on the other hand, did not fill his pockets or his satchel with gold. Instead, he picked up one large nugget. Light-footed, he rushed back to his village, announced his discovery to his friends, and returned with them and all the necessary equipment to mine the gold. He and his friends became the wealthiest people in the land.

Like the three travelers in the fable, you, too, have a choice of how to approach the information contained in this book. You may skim through it in order to learn of the immediate benefits, you might choose to apply what you learn in order to develop a lucrative, part-time career, or you might possess the unusual vision to see the enormous opportunities open to you in developing a large travel business. Only **you** can determine which approach fits you best.

WHO WILL BENEFIT FROM THIS BOOK

When I was first struck with the idea of writing this book, my intention was to compose a concise introductory report on outside sales. However, the more comprehensive my research became, the more I realized the need for a step-by-step manual on the subject. As it grew in scope, this "concise introductory report" sprouted its own wings and took flight as a full-fledged study on how to become a successful Travel Consultant. In addition to the general reader who is not yet acquainted with the travel industry, there are several groups of travel professionals who will gain vital knowledge by reading this book. (If you are new to the world of travel, reading this section is optional.) They are:

Travel Consultants

If you are already involved in the field of outside sales, you will benefit in the following ways:

• Since this is the first book to recognize outside sales as the important profession it is, as you read it, you will become filled with self-confidence and pride for having chosen such a wonderful career.

• Chapters five, six, and seven are chock-full of ideas and tips on how you can substantially increase your present travel business. Each one of these ideas can help you add thousands of dollars to your income.

• Feeling a bit stale? We all reach "valleys" in our work from time to time. With the help of this book, you may decide to set exciting new goals and generate more business than ever before.

• This book will help you to think **BIG.** Our treatment of the materials will enable you to see the Travel Consultant profession in its fullest scope. If you have never dared approach those "big accounts" before, perhaps now you will.

Inside Staff Travel Agents

We hope that many agents working inside the travel agency will read this book. Here's why:

• The rapid changes within the travel industry are posing new demands upon the individual travel counselor for which he or she may not be prepared. Most of the training that travel counselors receive is directed toward the knowledge of how to write tickets, how to use a computer, and how to book destinations and tours. While information of this sort is obviously essential, it does not, by itself, produce a single client. Today, successful agents must learn how to *sell* travel better. In order to ensure their continued growth within the travel business, they must learn the methods involved in generating new clients, while improving the retention rate of present customers. This book contains step-by-step, practical information on selling individual and group travel.

• As the field of outside sales assumes greater importance in many agencies, it is essential that the "inside staff" develops understanding and respect for the work performed in the field (and vice-versa). After all, the volume bonuses paid to the travel agencies from the airlines and cruise lines are a result of everyone's efforts—both "inside" and "outside."

Travel Agency Owners and Managers

Do you belong to the group of travel agency executives who has not yet developed a productive outside sales force? Are you wondering if having an outside sales staff would bring you more headaches instead of new business? The answer to these questions lies in the kind of program you design. We have seen many travel agencies who have an outside sales staff but who have spent very little time in designing an effective marketing program. As a result, they do not receive the maximum performance from their

11

Puerto Rico—At the Regent's Cerromar Beach Hotel, a reef protects swimmers on the crescent-shaped beach, while breakers froth their way to the surrounding area. Travel Consultants help couples like the one pictured to experience the beauty of the world's finest beaches.

outside sales force. On the other hand, those agencies that take the time to develop an ongoing training program, institute a strong marketing plan, execute clearly-set guidelines, and recruit well-motivated people see a dramatic increase in new business. This belief is not without support. Janet Farro, C.T.C., owner and manager of Long Shore Travel, Massapequa, Long Island, writes:

> Many travel agencies do not realize the full value to be obtained from efficient management of outside sales people. Personally, in this agency, following the implementation of an active outside sales force, a volume increase of 40% has been achieved. This increase has had little effect on the normal office routine and has added only a slight burden to the responsibilities of management.

Each year, the travel industry spends millions of dollars on lavish advertising campaigns. Airlines compete with one another, each trying to increase its market share. Cruise lines advertise to its two "bread and butter" groups: the older, affluent and the carefree singles. To a large degree, these carriers are "preaching in heaven"— selling travel to those who are already sold. But what about the majority who do not travel regularly? Because these individuals do not relate to travel advertising, they "tune it out." Here is where the one-on-one method of sales can outshine all other forms of promotion. The Travel Consultant can effectively reach the non-traveling public and the non-user of travel agencies. Here are some examples of market segments that you, as the owner/ manager of a travel agency, could not easily penetrate without a working outside sales staff:

• **Self-contained groups**—These can be fraternal orders, ethnic societies, church and religious organizations, trade associations, bowling leagues, doctors' wives, and other hard-to-reach clusters of people who prefer doing business with "their own." If you have a member of one of these groups on your outside sales staff, you will develop new markets with a huge potential for profits.

• **First-time travel agency clients**—There are millions of people who have never bought tickets through a travel agency. One reason is that many still suffer from the misconception that purchasing tickets in this manner will cost them more money. In order to overcome this prejudice, these individuals need the patient explanation of someone they trust—someone who will explain to them how a travel agency gets paid. Your Travel Consultant, who is *their* friend, will take the time to explain this. *You*, then, will receive new business.

• **The fear-of-flying group**—With 50% of our population yet to fly in an airplane, there is a vast untapped market of people who need special attention in order to help them overcome their fears and doubts about air travel. A patient and concerned Travel Consultant can help these people book their first trip with you.

Another reason why you, as an agency owner/manager, should implement a successful outside sales program is the increased flexibility in the work place brought about by the widespread use of computers. These amazing machines will soon make it unnecessary for many travel agency personnel to go to the office in order to transact business. With a modem-telephone hook-up, your booking agents can take care of all business transactions from their home computers, with only the support staff having to work at your agency. Because of this, within a few years, most agents will work outside the agency and, in essence, could be classified as "outside sales" people. This can mean that you, as an agency owner/manager, will have a large number of people on your staff who will rarely need to visit the home headquarters. The opportunities for increased volume can be enormous if you start **now** to prepare for this inevitable change. This book will help you gain an understanding of how to develop an outside sales force.

USING THIS BOOK AS A TEXTBOOK

This book should become mandatory reading for **all** those who are planning to enter the travel field. Why? Many courses in community colleges, universities, and travel schools do an excellent job in teaching the mechanics of the travel business. *Travel Free! How to Start and Succeed in Your Own Travel Consultant Business* will supplement that training with sales-oriented techniques to help the new "travel recruits" develop marketing know-how. In addition, the information contained herein is an excellent outline for a training course for new Travel Consultants in travel agencies.

HOW TO GET THE MOST FROM THIS BOOK

I would like to make the following suggestion to you. Use this as a workbook. Many people, when studying a book, are reluctant to write in it. It's probably a throwback to our school days when Miss Singleton would give us a demerit for marring the school property with our doodlings. (Did you ever do that?) This book was purposely designed to give you wide margins in which to write your notes and comments. Don't hesitate to use a yellow fluorescent pen to highlight important information. By doing this, you will absorb the material more thoroughly. If, while you're reading, an idea flashes its creative light, write it down. A well-marked book is the signature of a creative reader.

ACCOUNTABILITY

If you are new to the world of travel, you are about to discover exciting opportunities never before available to you. As you read this book, you will, no doubt, become enthusiastic about the many ways in which you will benefit from your new career. Before you read further, I would like to remind you of something of which you are probably already aware. No book, however informative, can make you successful. This is simply a blueprint—a map. It can point you in the right direction, as well as provide guidance. But the achieving is left to you. Even as your enthusiasm for a travel career grows, you may find your mind forming old excuses and dredging up out-worn alibis to help you rationalize why you will not be successful. (Many of us suffer from the "ugly duckling" self-image that succeeds in defeating us before we even start.) Don't let this happen to you. For once, discard the old thought habits that have kept you from achieving your full potential. This is a new day, a new opportunity. Act upon it!

The *Golden Odyssey*, Royal Cruise Lines' Greek-registered luxury cruise ship sailing the Mediterranean—You can qualify for free cruise travel by booking passengers on ships like the *Golden Odyssey*.

Virtue and vice, happiness and misery, are much more equally distributed to nations than those are permitted to suppose who have never been from home, and who believe, like the Chinese, that their residence is the center of the world, of light, of privilege, and of enjoyment.
AMASSA DELANO

CHAPTER TWO

THE
WORLD
OF TRAVEL

A BIT OF TRAVEL HISTORY

We take so much for granted. We just assume that all of the modern conveniences that we enjoy, from the automobile to the electric coffee maker, have always existed. It's even worse with our children. They "zap" extra-terrestrial beings on their video machines without a thought to the miracle of it all.

The same is true with travel. A businessman climbs into an airplane on the west coast, and five hours and five minutes later, he emerges in New York City, after having had a three-course dinner, a martini, and a two-hour nap. You'd think that he would scratch his head in wonderment and look up to heaven in thankful prayer for having just crossed the continent safely in so short a time. Not on your life! This fellow is cursing the airline because the plane arrived five minutes late!

Travel is as old as mankind. On that day when early man decided to leave his own hunting grounds and forage for bigger game elsewhere, he became a traveler. He was curious about the manners and habits of his neighbors and was awe-struck by the mysterious mountains and endless rivers which he encountered. As an old man, while squatting by the fire with his entranced offspring, he would repeatedly spin tales of his youthful travels.

For many centuries, relatively few people traveled beyond a day's journey on foot. Those who did venture outside their immediate surroundings were usually traveling for a good reason. These adventurous types might have been Greek soldiers marching to war against foreign enemies. (Alexander the Great and his army marched from Macedonia to the borders of India.) Perhaps they were merchants out to trade their local pottery in distant lands in return for spices and gold. The Phoenicians were famous throughout the ancient world for their great skill as seamen/traders. Their many ships were the envy of all for their speed and their ability to cross great distances. In the thirteenth century, the legendary Marco Polo was among those who were successful in crossing Asia by land and reaching China. We should all be grateful to merchants like him for closing the gap of understanding betweeen East and West. With the invention of the compass, the Atlantic Ocean became the next frontier. It was now possible, for those brave enough to try, to reach every part of the world by ship. Soon, daring soldiers, accompanied by fearless priests, reached the shores of America to colonize and to spread their faith.

With the exception of royalty, who, as early as the ancient Egyptians, maintained summer palaces, travel for pleasure did not exist. There are several reasons for this. First, travel was slow on foot or on horseback. It was also fraught with danger because of highwaymen and un-friendly natives. In addition, free time, something we also take for granted today, was not available to the masses.

A British Caledonian Airlines jumbo jet preparing for departure from its home base at London-Gatwick Airport—As your travel experience grows, you will become "at home" with airline schedules worldwide.

Most people toiled from sunrise to sunset in order to eke out a meager existence. It was roughly two hundred years ago that leisure travel became more common. In Europe, relatively good and safe roads made travel by coach faster and less dangerous. With the Machine Age came new inventions that greatly improved transportation. Among those inventions were the steamboat (of "Fulton's Folly") and the mighty railroad.

The rise of factories throughout Europe and America created new fortunes by an emerging class of entrepreneurs who had little or no history of money in their families. These people developed tremendous appetites for having the best. They would travel to Paris for new fashions and visit Italy to bask in its sunny climate. They would also congregate at such resorts as Baden Baden, in Germany, to partake of the hot-springs "cures" and to rub shoulders with the nobility (who still enjoyed more status in spite of their dwindling bank accounts).

The most profound change in people's thinking, however, occurred with the advent of the telegraph. Within a few years, news from other parts of the world, which had previously taken weeks and sometimes months to arrive, became almost instantly available. The world had suddenly become smaller. Now, every citizen had a way to be in touch with life outside his immediate town or village, and that stimulated his appetite to see more of the world. With the gradual improvement of working conditions and increased pay, more people could now take vacations and travel for pleasure.

In the early twentieth century, business travel and tourism gathered new momentum. Ocean liners, automobiles, and later, airplanes, were transporting more and more people at greater speed and convenience. It's hard to believe that civilian air travel is only fifty to sixty years old and that airplane travel has become commonplace only within the last twenty-five years. In 1960, for example, 1,634,000 passengers flew overseas from the United States. Twenty years later, that figure jumped to 8,163,000 passengers. And still, it is estimated that roughly 50% of the people in the United States have never been on an airplane! Travel, as we know it today, by millions of people, is a new field with tremendous potential—and much of that potential is still untapped.

But what about the future? Will people be traveling more or not as much? According to experts, current trends show greater cause for optimism than ever before. As computers and robots accomplish more of our menial tasks in the factory, office, and home, it is predicted that the average person will work fewer hours and will be better paid. With more money in their pockets and more time on their hands, how better will people enjoy these newly acquired freedoms than committing some of them to the joys of travel?

THE TRAVEL INDUSTRY —
HOW IT WORKS

In order to help you gain a better understanding of the components of the travel industry, five significant areas will be discussed. They are:

I. Passenger Transportation
II. Lodging
III. Cruises and Freighter Travel
IV. Wholesale Tour Operators
V. Travel Agencies

I. Passenger Transportation

Webster's New World Dictionary, Second College Edition, defines the term "transportation" as "the work or business of conveying passengers or goods." To a large extent, the primary preoccupation of all travel professionals is the transporting of people and their luggage from Point A to Point B and back again with the least amount of wear and tear. The Machine Age has created for us a variety of ways by which we can travel. Our decision as to which method of transportation we elect depends upon the amount of time we want to spend on traveling, the distance to be covered, and finally, our personal choice. The following industries are involved in transporting passengers from one destination to another:

★Railroads★

Once the preferred way of travel on land in America, our railroads are but a shadow of their glorious past. Railroads still do a significant job in transporting goods from one section of the country to another. But by 1980, passenger rail travel constituted less than 3% of all public transportation nationally. On May 1, 1971, Congress authorized the formation of Amtrak, the nation's new rail passenger system, with the goal to "get people back on trains." Thirteen years later, the debate still rages about the extent of the progress that has been made. In spite of the tortoise-like improvements, however, our dilapidated passenger train system appears to be on the mend (with your tax dollars and mine, naturally). In recent years, Amtrak, in an effort to increase passenger traffic, has been aggressively promoting the sale of train tickets through travel agents.

The sad condition of our rail system is in sharp contrast to the health of railroads elsewhere. In Japan and in western Europe, a thoroughly modern and efficient railway system provides a major means of transporting a constant stream of people. In Europe, national pride seems to hinge upon the state of the rail system. By 1981, the French, not to be outdone when their country's stature is at stake, had spent several billion dollars in order to perfect the TGV, the "fastest train in the world." This lightning-fast transport, which travels at the authorized rate of 170 m.p.h., is actually capable of racing at the world-record speed of 238 m.p.h.

Because of the much-touted convenience of the European railway system, many Europe-bound Americans purchase a Eurailpass. Eurail is the cooperative agency that unifies all of the different national rail systems of Europe. As long as they purchase it prior to their arrival in Europe, American tourists can buy an unlimited travel pass for a week, a month, or even longer periods. In 1982, more than 173,000 Eurailpasses with a value in excess of $55,000,000 were sold in North America. According to a market survey conducted by Eurail, the main reasons travelers decided to purchase these passes were:

- the flexibility of traveling wherever they want to go,
- the dependability and reliability of European trains,

24

The TGV—Train Grande Vitesse, the fastest train in the world, "flies" at more than twice the speed of ordinary trains. Trains are a great choice for your clients who wish to really see Europe.

- the advantage of sightseeing in complete comfort while viewing the countryside, and
- the pleasure of meeting the family people of Europe.

Ninety-five percent of all Eurailpasses are sold through travel agents. In addition to Eurail, several countries, such as Germany, Great Britain, and Switzerland, offer unlimited, all-inclusive train passes within their boundaries.

★Buses★

Bus companies account for 8.25% of the total public transportation in the United States. Most of this volume consists of the normal transportation of people from place to place by such companies as Greyhound and Trailways.

Although they are authorized to sell bus tickets, travel agents rarely handle this kind of standard bus travel. The more specialized forms of bus travel, however, play a significant and ever-growing role in the kind of services that travel agencies eagerly perform for their clients. Among these services are:

• **Tours** — Bus tours, usually lasting from three to seven days, are becoming increasingly popular, both here and abroad. The buses used for these trips, often called motor coaches, are usually quite luxurious. These tours provide an excellent and economical way for tourists to see the countryside without the burden of driving. The travelers also have the special privilege of being accompanied by an informed and friendly guide to educate and entertain them. This type of travel seems to be especially popular with our increasing population of older Americans. Because of recent deregulation of ground transportation, a boom in bus tours in the coming years is confidently predicted.

•**Local sightseeing** — Once they arrive in a new city, many people enjoy taking a guided bus tour of the most popular "spots." After all, what could be more convenient than seeing the sun-drenched beauties of Rome or Athens from the comfort of an air-conditioned bus? Local sightseeing excursions are an important ingredient in package tours. (Package tours are trips where the details and the itinerary have been pre-determined for a group of passengers.)

•**Shuttle buses** — Accurate information about bus transportation from the airport to his hotel destination is useful to any prudent traveler. But if you are leading a group of people on a trip, remember that the prior hiring of good and reliable local ground transportation waiting at the airport to take your clients to their hotel without hassles will add immeasurably to the success of your trip. Many an otherwise well-planned tour has been spoiled by a lack of attention to this crucial detail.

★Car Rental★

At one time, business travelers were the exclusive users of rental cars. After arriving by air to their destinations, they would rent a car at the airport and drive, map in hand, to their business appointments. Car rental agencies still do the majority of their transactions with these business travelers. But today, the concept of renting a car upon arrival at one's destination has become accepted by vacation travelers, as well. Once the "energy crunch" of the 1970s made it prohibitive for many to drive over long distances, the "fly-drive" method of vacation began to make a great deal of sense. In Hawaii, for example, a rental car is automatically included in many package trips. Today, it is estimated that roughly one-third of all airline passengers will rent a car upon arrival at their destinations. This business has become an important part of the transactions that travel agents handle and has boosted their income dramatically.

★Limousines★

Once the exclusive province of the very rich, chauffeured limousines are becoming an increasingly popular method of local travel by top corporate personnel and affluent vacationers. Busy executives, who have several appointments in their city of destination, have discovered the convenience of being taken directly to those appointments without having to worry about directions and parking. In addition, an executive can get a tremendous amount of work done in the back seat of a limousine. This, alone, can justify the extra cost. Affluent travelers, flying to a country whose language they may not speak, enjoy the luxury of having an English-speaking driver pick them up at the airport, take them to their hotel, show them the sights, and arrange for dinner at an excellent restaurant, without having to deal with the usual difficulties that can accompany foreign travel. In arranging a trip for a client, a Travel Consultant can effectively include a limousine service for those who wish it.

★Airlines★

The airlines clearly dominate the travel industry both nationally and internationally. In 1980, air travel constituted 89.5% of all public travel in America. The airlines can be divided into two separate groups: scheduled airlines and charter flights.

• **Scheduled airlines** — Over 90% of all air travel is done on regularly scheduled airlines. These carriers offer regular, time-table flights from city to city, crisscrossing both the United States and the world. Tickets for these flights can be purchased directly from the airlines or through a travel agency. Because of the great complexity and variety in air fares and rules today, approximately 70% of all airline tickets are bought from travel agencies and their representatives.

• **Charter flights** — Although their reputation was marred in the 1970s because of financial and scheduling problems created by unscrupulous operators, charter flights are again providing an alternative way of travel. Charters are primarily used by non-business travelers. Their greatest attraction is their substantially lower cost. Charter companies are able to provide more economical prices because they offer fewer flights than regularly scheduled airlines. This allows them to fill up their airplanes over a longer period of time. Another factor that contributes to their lower prices is that they service only the most heavily traveled destinations, such as London, Jamaica, and Hawaii.

Recent regulatory requirements by the Civil Aviation Board (C.A.B.) have eliminated all but the most ethical companies from the charter flight business. Today, the use of charters is as safe as that of regularly scheduled airlines. In addition, these new rulings have given the charter operators greater freedom in offering a variety of flight options to their passengers. Charter companies act as wholesalers, leaving the business of selling tickets at retail primarily to travel agencies and their representatives. Both scheduled airlines and charter flights can play a significant role in your career as a Travel Consultant.

II. Lodging

All commercial establishments which provide overnight accommodations are classified as "lodging." Some, like Motel 6, provide few amenities beyond a clean room. Others, such as La Costa Resort in southern California, provide everything from room and meals to tennis, golf, a health club, a weight-loss clinic, and much more.

At one time, very few people used hotels. When people traveled, they usually stayed with relatives or friends. It was in the 1950s that the trend began to change. With air travel on the rise, more individuals flew on business and needed a place to spend the night. Also, as vacationers became more affluent, they sought better and more standardized accommodations for themselves and their families. The phenomenal success story of Holiday Inns and Howard Johnson's was a result of fulfilling the need for good and predictable accommodations.

Another factor that has added immeasurably to the growth of the hotel-motel industry has been the rise of convention business. Groups with a common affinity began to look for exciting locations in which to meet for their annual conventions. Moreover, large corporations began to hold regular meetings at hotels, preferring to rent the space on a one-shot basis rather than to build additional meeting rooms themselves. Addressing themselves to the seemingly insatiable appetite for hotel space, giants such as Hilton, Sheraton, Marriott, and Hyatt began to emerge. Unlike the more regulated airlines, hotels have almost unlimited freedom to negotiate prices on an individual or group basis. This will be of great benefit to you in negotiating prices for group travel and conventions. Hotel space is sold directly to the consumer or through a travel agent.

III. Cruises and Freighter Travel

You might be wondering why I chose to list cruises and freighters separately. After all, isn't a ship a form of transportation? Of course it is. But today, the primary function of a cruise ship is that of a floating resort hotel.

Until the 1960s, the main purpose of passenger ships was to transport people from one destination to another. Luxury liners, such as the legendary *Titanic*, the *Bismarck*, the *Ile de France*, the *United States*, and the *Queen Mary*, crisscrossed the Atlantic, providing the only form of passenger transportation between Europe and America. Predictably, as air travel became a safe, swift, and inexpensive way to travel, the passenger ship companies went through a major identity crisis. Many people began to see the beautiful big ships as dinosaurs of a bygone, though glorious age. But they were wrong. In the late 1960s, in a brilliant stroke of marketing genius, the steamship companies turned the bows of their beautiful vessels southward to the Caribbean and the Mediterranean. Instead of offering point-to-point destinations, as in the past, the cruise lines developed luxury cruises that started and ended in the same port. For example, a seven-day Caribbean cruise on one of these lovely ships might start in Miami, continue to San Juan, St. Thomas, Port-au-Prince, the Grand Cayman Islands, and then return to Miami. This kind of travel has become extremely popular. Aided by the long-running television show, "The Love Boat," passenger volume tripled in the 1970s to more than a million a year. In 1983, the total is estimated to have reached 1.7 million. On a cruise, passengers can travel in great luxury, be fed seven times a day, go to nightclubs, meet others, and still be able to sightsee in varying locales during day excursions—all this without having to pack and unpack their luggage.

Today, cruising continues to be a very big business. Cruise lines operate all over the world, often filled to capacity with satisfied, and I might add, over-fed vacationers. (A friend of ours, having recently returned from a fourteen-day cruise, confided to us, "I came aboard as a passenger, and I got off as excess baggage.") To date, only 5% of Americans have ever sailed on a cruise, a fact that should make you reel with excitement about the potential out there. Cruise travel, one of the most profitable areas in the industry, can be extremely lucrative for the ambitious Travel Consultant.

Another way available to travel by sea is aboard a freighter. The International Conventions and Conferences on Marine Safety defines the freighter or cargo liner which carries passengers as "a vessel principally engaged in transporting goods, which is licensed to carry a maximum of twelve passengers." There are several reasons why some prefer traveling by freighters. Here are just a few:

● **Total relaxation** — With few fellow passengers and an unstructured day, you can unwind in an informal atmosphere.

- **Adventure** — On a freighter, passengers experience life at sea as it really is. Although the accommodations on a freighter are often more luxurious than those on a cruise ship (surprised?), you have the opportunity of seeing the crew at work. You can even imagine being an "old salt" yourself because you have almost complete run of the ship while on board.

- **Lower cost** — The cost of traveling by freighter is often half as much as that of a luxury liner with comparable accommodations.

- **Smooth sailing** — Freighters provide unusually smooth sailing. One reason is that the cargo carried at the bottom of the freighter acts as a stabilizer. The wide beam of freighters also tends to reduce any tendency of rolling.

Booking passengers on freighters is often done by travel agents. A few travel agencies have even made a point of specializing in this form of travel. There are, however, a few drawbacks to traveling by freighter. One must set aside a large block of time for travel, since freighters follow their own leisurely course as they load and unload their cargo in exotic, out-of-the-way ports. Also, the total number of spaces available on freighters is quite limited, making it necessary for bookings to be made months in advance. Is freighter travel for everyone? Obviously not, but it does claim its aficionados who wouldn't go to sea any other way.

IV. Wholesale Tour Operators

Traveling abroad involves many details. A typical vacation to Europe would include, at the minimum, airline transportation, hotel accommodations, meals, and local sightseeing. Many people, wishing to enjoy a carefree vacation, prefer to leave the details of their trip to others. Tour operators cater to these individuals by providing them with a pre-planned, escorted tour. How do tour operator companies differ from travel agencies? Acting as a *wholesaler*, a tour operator contacts the hotels, local attractions, ground transportation companies, and other businesses and individuals whose services are needed for the tour's success and then assembles, or packages, them into a unified whole. The tour operator, in turn, advertises and sells these tours primarily through retail travel agencies.

Since it would be prohibitively expensive to arrange such a tour for one individual, tour operators create vacation trips on a group basis. By choosing itineraries and programs that would appeal to many, they are able to sell space on each tour until they meet their quota and sell out. Convenience is not the only reason that many people prefer traveling en masse. Often, one can save money by going on a tour. Because the tour operators, as wholesalers, buy in bulk, they receive "preferred" rates on the different components that make up the tour. In many cases, these savings are reflected in the package price paid by the passenger. Another appealing feature of group travel is companionship. Many enjoy traveling in the company of "kindred spirits"—people with similar interests. The shared adventures experienced on a group tour provide a natural setting for friendship and camaraderie.

Today, there are literally hundreds of tour operators and thousands of tours from which to choose. These tours range from the introductory, tightly structured, whirlwind, if-it's-Tuesday-it-must-be-Belgium variety to the leisurely, semi-structured, meandering type geared to the "veddy" sophisticated. (One tour operator offers the "lazyman's tour"—twenty-eight nights in one Swiss location.) Tours are planned according to varying needs and interests. Some are designed for young marrieds, others for mature singles. You can get a bird's-eye view of southern France from a hot-air balloon, or you may test your machismo on a safari in Kenya. Do you have an interest in antiques, books, auto races, jewelry, horses, music, treasure hunting, gourmet foods, golfing, religion, collecting seashells, marathon running, bird watching, or Indian mysticism? Somewhere, there's a tour just right for you!

Tour packages are one of the staple items of a travel agency. One of the reasons is that they provide most, if not all, of the client's travel needs. This makes the travel agent's job much easier than having to book each segment of a client's trip individually. As a new Travel Consultant, recommend only those trips that are handled by the most reputable tour operators. Your travel agency will, no doubt, have a list of those with whom they have had a satisfactory relationship.

V.   Travel Agencies

In 1841, a young man approached officials of Midland Counties Railway Company with an idea. "Why not run a special train between Leicester and Loughborough for the temperance meeting to be held on July 5?" he asked. The train officials were more than a little dubious. After all, such an idea had never been tried before. But Thomas Cook was persistent, and his persuasive manner finally prevailed. The train was run, and the experiment was a success. This was the beginning of Thomas Cook and Son, the first travel agency. It was also the start of a new and exciting profession.

Just what is a travel agent, anyway? Travel agents are professional counselors on travel to the public. They help plan trips, book hotel rooms, sell airline tickets, and take care of the myriad travel arrangements for their clients.

In order for a travel agency to be officially appointed by the airlines and other suppliers, it must meet several qualifications with regard to finances and retail travel experience. Travel agents must agree to abide by certain standards of ethics. They must also maintain an office which is used exclusively for the sale of travel arrangements or travel-related services. For some reason, many people still believe that they have to pay an additional fee for these services. This is not the case. Instead, travel agencies are paid a commission by the airlines, hotels, cruise lines, wholesale tour operators, and car rental companies. The rate of the commission varies. But broadly, the commission structure is as follows:

- Airlines: 8% to 11%
- Hotels: 10% to 20%
- Cruise Lines: 10% to 15%
- Wholesale Tour Operators: 10% to 18%
- Car Rental Companies: 10% to 30%

In addition to these commissions, agencies that attain volume quotas set by these suppliers qualify to receive overrides. These additional bonuses can add as much as 80% to the agency's commission. Many travel agencies share these bonuses with the inside and outside staff members who contribute to the qualifying volumes.

In the past, consumers could rely on standardized airline ticket prices between two cities, regardless of which airline they used. In contrast, the present situation can be bewildering. The deregulation of the airlines industry by the federal government has created a very competitive atmosphere. Each carrier has several price categories for the same flight in order to compete head-on with rival airlines. For example, on the same flight from Philadelphia to San Francisco, you can reserve the same seat in coach class under several different designations.

The difference between a full-fare coach ticket, excursion fare, and "super saver" can be measured in hundreds of dollars, with absolutely no difference in service! As a result, all but the most experienced traveler have become dependent upon the travel agent's services. This dependency has helped to stimulate a tremendous proliferation of new travel agencies. In the past fifteen years, their number has more than quintupled to approximately 23,000 in the United States and 3,000 in Canada.

At this writing, in order to be able to represent most domestic airlines, a travel agency must be approved by the Air Traffic Conference (A.T.C.). This organization is an association of airlines which has been established by the Civil Aeronautics Board to set the rules governing travel agents. For the sale of international airline tickets, a travel agency must be approved by I.A.T.A., the International Air Transport Association. I.A.T.A. is, in essence, a cartel of airline companies which sets rules and attempts to fix prices on the international routes. In addition to these, there are other licensing conferences. As the representative of the steamship companies, the Trans-Pacific Passenger Conference (T.P.P.C.) and the International Passenger Ship Association (I.P.S.A.) act in a similar fashion.

Although the travel agency business boasts its own giants, such as American Express, Ask Mr. Foster, and E.F. MacDonald, with thousands of employees each, the average travel agency is a small operation. Most travel agencies have from two to ten employees, with annual sales ranging from $500,000 to $3,000,000 per year.

TOURISM—WHY DO PEOPLE TRAVEL?

Anyone sitting at one of the international air terminals at Kennedy Airport in New York City during the first week of September is bound to witness an unforgettable sight. Thousands of Americans—young and old; alone or with children; disheveled; their clothing well-worn; carrying bulging suitcases while receiving an incessant, rhythmic thrashing from their strapped-on cameras—are coming home. Why did these people leave the comfort and security of their cities, towns, and villages and brave foreign languages, fluctuating exchange rates, and a possible case of diarrhea? Why do others endure the cramped discomfort of campers and take to the open roads of our super highways? Travel seems to answer a number of the needs of mankind. Here are some of the reasons why people travel:

• **Travel fulfills dreams.**— For many of us, our most cherished dream is the desire to travel. Some people have a specific place they want to go. For Nancy's mother, her dream has always been to go to Hawaii. For another relative, a trip to the Holy Land beckons. For you, it may be a chance to visit your ancestral home in the "old country." Television has done much to instill dreams in the hearts of its viewers. In addition to "The Love Boat," "Hawaii Five-O," "Magnum P.I.," and "Fantasy Island," many of the adventure-type series, such as "Hart to Hart," have shot episodes in exotic locations throughout the world. Some experts contend that television has done more to stimulate the desire to travel than any other medium.

• **Travel offers a welcome change.**—There is much truth in the cliché, "Variety is the spice of life." And travel, as if by magic, allows us to alter our surroundings. By the time your jet lands in a resort island in the Caribbean, your cares and responsibilities, which had seemed so important a few hours before, are reduced to little more than a dim memory. You are now ready to unwind and "let loose." Travel provides a bridge from the routine to the extraordinary, from work to play, from responsibility to pleasure.

• **Travel is an investment in memories.**—Long after we take a trip, we receive residual pleasure from the recollection of our adventures. Our photographs and slides help to evoke the memories of people we met and places we visited. Travel is a wonderful way to strengthen family ties and enhance friendships, as we recall again and again our shared discoveries and misadventures.

• **Travel recharges our batteries.**—New experiences and a change of pace allow us to set new goals, tap our creative juices, and develop youthful enthusiasm for new and unfinished tasks. After returning home recently from a wonderful vacation at the Kapalua Bay Hotel on the island of Maui—one of the world's finest resorts—we were so filled with energy, that we were able to complete one month's projects in seven days!

• **Travel educates us and widens our horizons.**— After viewing the world through our nineteen-inch video screen, travel gives us a true perspective on the wondrous world we inhabit. There is no substitute for personally experiencing the vastness of the Grand Canyon or seeing a Da Vinci original in the Louvre or scuba diving in the Gulf of Eilat (Israel). Travel also gives us great perspective in yet another way. If we are sensitive, we realize how universal is the human condition; we all seek the same things—love, understanding, security, and freedom of expression.

• **Travel helps us to become more confident.**— Removed as we are when we travel from our familiar and safe environment, we are forced to draw upon dormant inner resources. As we manage to survive new and unusual circumstances, we become more independent. This helps us to gain renewed self-assurance in our ability to cope.

• **Travel can take us back to our roots.**—We, in America, are a people of immigrants. Most of our family trees can be traced elsewhere. Whether it's Joe Agresti traveling to Rome, Lynne Chan visiting Hong Kong, Miriam Levy traveling to Jerusalem, or Steven McPherson visiting his Celtic ancestors in Edinburgh, people have an insatiable curiosity about their roots. Travel gives us the chance to bridge the cultural gap between past, present, and future. And for many of us, this infuses new meaning and depth into our lives.

• **Travel can rekindle relationships.**—There are times when the routine of life can suffocate our capacity to feel. Travel, like a current of fresh air, can breathe new life into a tired relationship. The balding and uncommunicative "old man" becomes as ardent as a Latin lover in May. The "good ol' Mom" is transformed into a youthful and sultry temptress. Many a rut-filled marriage of stale habits has received a much-needed charge on a journey away from home.

• **Travel satiates our wanderlust.**—Are you a frustrated Robinson Crusoe or an armchair Columbus? Have you ever dreamed of crossing new oceans or hiking the Himalayas? Travel allows us to fulfill our need to explore and to discover. As we wind our way to the top of the Canadian Rockies to feast our unbelieving eyes on the magnificent view of Lake Louise before us, it's fun to fantasize that we are the first to "discover" one of nature's masterpieces.

• **Travel helps us to appreciate home.**—As much as we enjoy our "getaway," travel gives us greater appreciation for what we have. No American or Canadian can appreciate his country fully until he goes abroad. And, as we enter our home, humble as it may be, returning to familiar surroundings and the loving arms of family and friends, we are filled with new appreciation of our unique place in this vast and wonderful world.

Done with indoor complaints, libraries, querulous criticisms, Strong and content I travel the open road.
WALT WHITMAN

CHAPTER THREE

YOUR CAREER IN OUTSIDE SALES

THE MANY WAYS TO SELL TRAVEL

As a self-employed Travel Consultant, you will enjoy an unusual amount of freedom and flexibility. You will have the opportunity to decide how much time you want to spend on your career and when you wish to call on your clients. Other questions that you will want to answer are:

• Do I want to service individual travelers, develop group and corporate sales, or perhaps do a mixture of both?

• With how much of the actual travel preparations, such as writing tickets and making reservations, do I wish to be involved?

In order to illustrate some options you have as a beginner in the travel industry, I shall relate the stories of two Travel Consultants who have developed successful part-time businesses.

Janet's Story

Janet is a dedicated school teacher and is well known in her community. She is married, has three children, and is a valued member of several civic groups. A few years ago, Janet heard from a friend about the opportunities in outside sales, and she became enthusiastic. According to Janet, "Here was an opportunity for me to help other people while making extra money and receiving several thousands of dollars worth of travel benefits. I just couldn't pass up the chance." Janet then contacted the largest travel agency in her city of approximately 100,000 people and began her career as a Travel Consultant strictly on a part-time basis.

First, she made a list of her friends, relatives, neighbors, and colleagues and let them know that she had just become a Travel Consultant. After explaining what a Travel Consultant does, Janet asked them for their commitment to book all of their travel services through her. It was surprisingly easy to receive this commitment, since the majority of the people on her list did not possess a strong relationship with a travel agency. A few people seemed to be concerned about the cost of her services until Janet hastened to explain that they were free of charge. Furthermore, she made a strong selling point out of her willingness to deliver travel tickets to her customers' homes or places of work.

Now, every month, Janet sends her clients/friends a brief newsletter informing them of new travel opportunities and any good "buys." She also adds a personal "blurb" or two about those clients who just came back from a trip, often including "wacky" pictures from their recent vacations—Mary sitting on a burro, Michael hanging from a cliff—that sort of thing. Every sixty days, Janet calls her clients (she now services 100 families) to ask if they have plans for any trips in the near future. If they do, she takes down the pertinent information. She has now made another sale. According to Janet, "Outside sales has been great. With teachers' salaries being what they are, I have been able to give myself a nice raise. Also, after my first year, my travel agency put me on their list as being eligible for travel discounts. As a result, for the past four years, Bill and I have been able to go on cruises, which we love, at least once a year. We couldn't afford to do this otherwise. But at $210 per person for a week's luxury cruise in the Caribbean [her cost with the travel agent's discount] instead of $1,400 per person, who can afford *not* to go?"

John's Story

John is a retired army major who specializes in group trips. Perhaps it would be more accurate to say that John's specialty has consisted of one trip a year. His story is typical of many of his age group who have become Travel Consultants. An energetic man, John was fast becoming bored with his retirement and disgusted with his monthly government paycheck. One evening, he, along with his wife, attended a neighborhood barbecue, where he met a travel agent. When the agent found out that John belongs to a fraternal organization, she told him about the opportunities for booking group travel in outside sales. "Don't worry about the details," she said. "Just get your organization to agree to sponsor one trip a year, and I will help you with the rest." A bit dubious, John made an appointment at the club and presented the idea to the executive committee. After some deliberation, the idea was approved unanimously. Many of the other members also agreed that here was a terrific way for friends and their wives to vacation together. John was excited! With the help of his travel agency, he became the tour organizer. Last year, 143 people went on the annual trip, this time to Germany and Switzerland. As a tour leader, John was able to arrange for both him and his wife to travel, all expenses paid. In addition to that, John's commission check for organizing the trip exceeded 50% of his retirement income! He is now planning to expand his travel business by calling on other organizations. "Why stop now?" says John. "This is fun!"

These are the stories of two Travel Consultants, who, like many, have developed their own part-time travel businesses. There are others who have chosen to build full-time careers in outside sales. One woman we met at a travel trade show in Reno sold her travel agency in order to launch a career in outside sales. "When I had my own agency," she disclosed, "all my profit was eaten by the constant overhead. After paying salaries and other expenses, there wasn't much left. In outside sales, I don't have the problems of running an agency, and the commission check is all mine." When we urged her further, she confided to us that she expected to earn between $38,000 to $41,000 this year. Some top Travel Consultants, many with their own staffs, claim to generate as much as $5,000,000 in sales each year—much more than most agencies. These people prefer not to run a full-fledged agency, with its paperwork and overhead. Instead, they opt to concentrate on selling travel one hundred percent of the time. For these top pros, gross incomes in the six figures are not unusual.

WHAT ARE THE QUALIFICATIONS TO START AS A TRAVEL CONSULTANT?

If you are enthusiastic about the idea of selling travel and are motivated to produce results, you are qualified to start your career as a Travel Consultant. With proper guidance, you can begin without further experience. This does not mean that you will not need to expand your

The Hotel Ritz garden-restaurant in Paris combines 18th century elegance with trees and flowers. This is where affluent Paris-bound travelers can be seen "putting on the Ritz."

knowledge as you work on gaining that experience. On the contrary, there is a great deal to learn. But your enthusiasm and eagerness in selling travel to a new client will be more important, initially, than knowing how to write a ticket or how to read the O.A.G. (Official Airlines Guide). Remember, the travel agency with which you work has plenty of people who know all about the mechanics of writing tickets. What the agency needs are bright, enthusiastic people like you who are willing to see the public and generate new accounts.

When Nancy and I booked our first convention for a travel agency, we knew next to nothing about the travel business. In fact, we were a bit nervous about the whole thing. But our agent did not seem to mind helping us with the paperwork for the business we generated. On the contrary, when we brought in a travel package consisting of 230 people, he grinned at us like a Cheshire cat.

WHO CAN BECOME
A TRAVEL CONSULTANT?

By now, it should be clear to you that **anyone** can be a Travel Consultant. Are you still having a difficult time putting yourself in the picture? Perhaps the following will help. Here are some of the categories of people who have done very well in the outside sales field:

Housewives

Outside sales is an ideal occupation for you if you are a housewife. You can work from your home and set your own hours. For the woman with children, married or single, here is a bona fide opportunity to help the family budget, develop an exciting new career, and reduce the costs of travel and vacation, without leaving home to go to a full-time job.

Sitmar Cruises' *Fairsea,* on a leisurely cruise through the majestic inside passage of Alaska—Sea and mountains blend in harmony as the snow-capped mountains are reflected on the icy water.

Corporate and Government Employees

Today, more and more corporate and government employees are seeking meaningful sidelines. Some are looking for a business of their own, while others are simply interested in supplementing their earnings. The field of outside travel sales is an exciting and lucrative way to develop part-time income. It is also a very smart way for you to gain expertise in the travel field, should you decide, at some time in the future, to start your own travel agency or wholesale tour company.

Retired People

Becoming a Travel Consultant is the ideal occupation for the retired man, woman, or couple. Here is a chance for you to turn your leisure time into productive use.

47

Since one of the main segments of vacation travelers is the senior citizen group, you can take care of your friends' travel needs and perhaps even qualify for free vacations yourself. At the same time, you will be supplementing your retirement income. Besides, getting involved again will be a wonderful way to add new meaning and zest to your life.

Volunteers and Civic-Oriented People

Are you a volunteer? Do you take part in community activities? Then you are a special person. Since you obviously enjoy being of value to others, you would, therefore, cultivate a large following of satisfied clients. Your desire to serve others can be turned into a wonderful service-oriented career in travel.

Ethnic Group Members

Because of cultural and linguistic problems, there are millions of people living in North America who are isolated from the rest of society. Yet, this growing segment of the population represents a huge potential market. Filipinos, Japanese, Russians, Egyptians, South Americans, Vietnamese, Cubans, Chinese, Portuguese, and Mexicans are just some of the ethnic groups that reside in our great country. If you are a member of one of these groups, you can provide a much-needed service to your people by helping them with their travel needs.

Church Groups

Are you a member of a church or synagogue? Have you always dreamed of going on a pilgrimage to the Holy Land, visiting the Vatican in Rome, or seeing the passion plays in Germany? Have you thought that you could never afford to go? Well, here is your chance! By organizing a group of people in your church or synagogue to go on a tour with you, you may have your trip paid for.

Club Members

Like John, our retired military officer, why don't you become the tour organizer for your club? In chapter seven, you will learn exactly what to do.

Sales People

With previous sales experience, you can do extremely well as a Travel Consultant. After all, what product could be more glamorous to sell than travel? Since more and more people are traveling, your "prospect list" is unlimited. Besides, you know how to close a sale, don't you? Perhaps you are involved in real estate or insurance sales and are looking for a fresh new start. Even if you are busy with your current career, diversifying one's income has never hurt anyone.

Students

Brian, an acquaintance of ours, started as a Travel Consultant while he was still in college. He did so well that his travel agency asked him to escort some groups. After graduation, he became a full-time travel agent. Today, he is in charge of the outside sales department of this large regional agency. If you are a student, think of all your friends who travel abroad, fly home to visit their folks, or go on weekend skiing vacations.

Mangrove Bay, Bermuda—Put yourself in the picture! White sands, balmy weather, crystal clear water, a sailboat, and you....

Couples

Have you been looking for a business where both you and your spouse can work together? Outside sales is ideal. Each one of you has your own set of strengths. One of you might be good at organizing and taking care of details. The other can excel in getting new accounts and servicing them. If this kind of arrangement can work for you, you are, in effect, doubling your productivity by working with your mate. Who knows? You may also be providing a new spark to your marriage. Nancy and I have certainly enjoyed, during the course of our married life, working on projects together.

Second Income Seekers

As more people find that their primary job is no longer enough to pay the bills and to get ahead, "moonlighting" (working for a second income) has become a worldwide phenomenon. Outside sales is an excellent way to bring in this extra income. You can visit your clients in their home in the evening, which is most convenient for them, and you can also conduct your business on the weekends. In addition, you will now be able to afford, at greatly reduced rates, to take memorable vacations.

Get the picture? Now, let's show you how to put **you** in the picture.

THE THREE TYPES OF TRAVEL CONSULTANTS

There are three different ways that you can operate your business as a Travel Consultant. The first two methods do not require that you have much knowledge about travel, while the third one does. As you begin to prosper in outside sales, you will probably develop greater expertise in all facets of the travel industry. Gradually, you will study and learn enough to reach the fullest level of professionalism.

The "Free Travel" Category

This can be a good way for you to establish a track record with a travel agency. Here is how it works. Organize a group of 10 or 15 friends and associates (5-8 couples) who wish to take a cruise or trip with you. After getting a strong indication of interest from them, visit a travel agency and ask to see the owner. Explain that you want to develop a career in outside sales. Tell him that as an example of your abilities, you would like to book this trip through his agency. All you want in return is to be the tour conductor (or tour escort) and to get all your expenses paid for. The travel agent should be delighted. First, his agency will receive and keep the full commission income. Second, your free tickets will be paid by the airline or cruise company. While policies differ somewhat from company to company, many cruise lines offer one free cruise for each 10 or 15 cruises that are sold to a group, while many airlines offer a free pass for each 15 tickets sold.

Have you wondered how you could ever go on a nice vacation on your present budget? So many people have dreams of travel that are never fulfilled. What a tragedy! If you do nothing more than arrange for a small group to travel with you, you could make that dream come true **right now!**

The "Finder" Category

"Finders" get new accounts and bring them to the travel agency with whom they work. This is their primary role. They differ from the "free travel" category in that they receive not only free travel for organizing a group but also a commission. They are also paid for all individual travel they book through their agency, even if it consists of one ticket sold to a single client. Finders are not usually involved in the writing of airline tickets. Janet, our ambitious school teacher, is an example of a finder. While she services approximately 100 families with their travel needs, she's content to allow her travel agency write the tickets. Because the paperwork is left to the agency, Janet is free to pursue what she does best— service her clients. Many people in outside sales are classified as "finders." They create individual and group clients from among their friends, relatives, and associates. They also establish accounts with businesses, associations, and clubs. Finders are of great benefit to travel agencies if they bring a large amount of new business. Those finders who create group and corporate travel accounts—whether for 10 or 500 people—are particularly sought after.

You can make good money as a finder. Finders are usually compensated anywhere from 20% to 50% of the commission received by the travel agency for any business they generate. Travel agencies average about 10% in commissions. Based on that, about 2% to 5% of the total price of the ticket, excluding tax, would go to you as a finder. Are you a bit confused? Don't be; it's quite simple. Let's say that you have arranged for a group of 30 people to go on a seven-day Caribbean cruise. The cost per person, including air fare, is $1,200 plus tax. First, because you have 30 people going, you and your spouse travel free as "tour conductors." That's a savings to you of $2,400 (2 free passes at $1,200 each). If you are paid 40% of the travel agency's commission, and the agency receives 10% from the cruise company, you can calculate your earnings as follows:

1) $1,200 per cruise × 30 people
   × 10% agency commission
   = $3,600.

2) $3,600 agency commission × 40% finder's commission
   = $1,440.

3) $1,440—finder's commission
   $2,400—free cruise value
   $3,840—your total earnings.

How's that for organizing a nice vacation for yourself and your friends, co-workers, relatives, or club members?

The Professional Travel Consultant Category

After you develop your career as a finder-type Travel Consultant and start making a good profit through your list of clients, you will want to learn more about all aspects of the travel business. At this point, you may be already engaged in outside sales as your main occupation. The next step for you would be to learn how to write airline tickets and to make reservations directly for your clients. To do this, you will want to take certain courses. If you are extremely lucky, your travel agency may have its own in-house training, but this is still rare. Many local colleges and trade schools, however, have a travel department as a part of their adult education program. In addition, the American Society of Travel Agents (A.S.T.A.) has a correspondence course (see Appendix).

Becoming fully proficient will have several advantages for you. First, you will become less dependent on the inside staff at your agency. This will aid you in processing more business and in servicing your clients better. (Travel Consultants can now arrange to have the complete Official Airlines Guide—O.A.G.—screened on their home computers. With a telephone hook-up, they can even make all reservations directly with the carriers without having to contact their agencies.) Because you are doing more of the work, you will now qualify for income ranging from 45% to 60% of the agency's commission. At 60%, the commission income you would make will be fifty percent more than that of a finder who receives a 40% commission. The difference in income is even more dramatic for the finder who is accustomed to getting 20% of the commission. At 60%, that Travel Consultant would triple his income. Some travel courses teach the ticketing aspect of the travel business in one or two sessions. For this kind of increase in your income, it will be well worth your time to enroll in one of these programs.

As someone who is new to the travel business, you may feel that reaching this level of expertise is a long way off. I understand how you feel. When we began to organize trips, the many details involved seemed overwhelming. If you had asked Nancy, before we embarked on our first convention tour, which she would rather do—organize group travel or run the Boston Marathon—I'm not sure what she would have answered. But like anything new, after awhile, coordinating a trip became a simple matter of handling one small detail after another. It's a bit like eating an elephant—we do it one bite at a time.

I should like to spend the whole of my life in traveling abroad, if I could anywhere borrow another life to spend afterwards at home.
WILLIAM HAZLITT

CHAPTER FOUR

THE MARVELOUS BENEFITS

The business of travel provides a dimension that is present in very few industries. That dimension is glamour. Who hasn't dreamed of fabulous vacations in romantic parts of the world? Visions of skiing in St. Moritz, motoring along the coastline of the French Riviera, sunbathing in Jamaica, or riding atop a camel near the pyramids of Egypt are so enticing. As a little boy, I devoured every issue of the *National Geographic* from cover to cover. A young Walter Mitty, I would fantasize about going on daring safaris, climbing the Himalayas, and touring the great castles on the Rhine. The lure of travel beckons to anyone who has an adventurous soul. Now, let's "explore" the possibilities of how you can make your travel fantasies a reality within the framework of your new career.

ESCORTING—TOUR CONDUCTING

The benefit of escorting was briefly touched upon in chapter three. Whenever you arrange for a group of people to travel together, you may qualify to be a tour conductor. This is how it works. The airlines, cruise lines, and tour companies understand that whenever a group of people travels together, it is essential that someone be assigned to the group to take care of their travel needs. This person is known as an escort, tour conductor, or tour leader. In order to promote travel and as a courtesy to travel agencies, these travel companies offer a free trip for each 10, 15, or 20 people traveling. (Each airline, cruise line, and tour company has its own policy, so it's important to check in advance.) For example, if you arrange for a group of 30 of your co-workers to vacation with you in Hawaii and the airline you choose provides one free ticket for each 15 tickets sold, you and your spouse may be able to travel without having to pay for your transportation. We know of a clergyman who arranged for a group of his church members to visit the Holy Land. For organizing the trip, he and his wife were able to have all of their travel expenses paid for. The trip was so successful that he is planning another one for this year. In New York City, in fact, there is a large travel agency that specializes in Holy Land tours which has a nation-wide network of clergy acting as Travel Consultants. This is a good time to mention an important point. If you are interested in escorting a group of your own, make sure that you have an agreement with your travel agency that assigns you as the tour leader for the trip. This way, no misunderstanding will occur.

Travel agencies often hire people as escorts to handle their own organized tours and convention business. For example, if the agency has developed a package tour to Tahiti, it needs a responsible person or couple to take care of all the details—everything from baggage handling and making sure that Mrs. Cohen is served a Kosher meal on the plane, to reminding a sleepy concierge of the welcome cocktail party that is due to begin in thirty minutes. Once you, as a Travel Consultant, have arranged for your own group trip and have proven yourself capable of handling the many details, your travel agency may ask you to act as an escort for some of their other tours. In those circumstances, where you escort the agency's tours rather than your own, you may be paid a per diem (daily allowance) by your agency. This per diem, which traditionally ranges from $25 to $100 per person per day, is paid, in addition, of course, to your travel expenses. If you enjoy escorting and taking care of the needs of people and if you are an organized, take-charge type of person, you may find yourself frequently jetting around the world as a tour conductor.

Organizing a trip among your friends and leading your agency's scheduled tours are certainly two excellent ways for you to participate in tour conducting. But there is yet another way. If you happen to speak a foreign language, be well acquainted with a particular country or region, or have an interest or background that can become the basis for a tour, you may be able, with the help of your travel agency, to plan an itinerary custom-made to your specialty. There are hundreds of possibilities for a "theme tour." For instance, do you have a knowledge of or special interest in archaeology, mountain climbing, wines, art history, opera, the Bible, bicycling, botany, zoology, fishing and game, trains, high fashion, golf, architecture, World War II history, primitive cultures, summer music festivals, antiques, or gourmet foods? If so, then you are a likely candidate for heading a tour of your own. In those circumstances where you are leading the tour and are also the "personality" around which the trip is built, you can arrange to share in the profits. This is done by adding a special fee for your services to the price of the package. Developing and organizing this kind of tour can be extremely lucrative. Theme travel has tremendous potential because there are many people who will only travel when their interests and hobbies are the central focus of the trip.

Escorting is an enticing travel alternative for anyone who is willing to accept the many responsibilities involved. But for two groups of people, in particular, it stands out as being an ideal occupation. One group is the retired, yet vigorous, who seek new excitement and additional income; the other consists of those involved in the teaching profession for whom escorting can be a splendid way to fill the summer months with travel adventure. Baxter Geeting is Professor Emeritus at the California State University in Sacramento. He and his wife, Corinne, have led numerous tours to Europe, the U.S.S.R., South America, and the Far East. With three young boys and a professor's salary, acting as tour leaders was their personal solution to the universal problem: How can we afford to travel? In their marvelously witty book, *Confessions of a Tour Leader,* Baxter and Corinne summarize the rewards of their many years of leading group tours this way:

> I think of the thrill of seeing, from my hotel balcony in Interlaken, the snowcapped Jungfrau at sunset on one of those rare days when she is naked to the view, not a hint of cloud to mar her pristine splendor.
>
> I think of the sensuous beauty of the Taj Mahal by moonlight. Of the matchless elegance of the Alhambra, sunlight filtering through marble lace. Of the lavish brilliance of shrines and temples of Nikko against the cool green Japanese cedars. Of the mountaintop sanctuary of the ancient Inca rulers, Machu Picchu, with its magnificent ruins of temples and terraced gardens. Of the overwhelming art collection in the old Winter Palace, known as the Hermitage, in Leningrad.

In reverie, they crowd my mind with color, with sound, with endless enchantment—these magic moments I have known.

They are the rewards of travel.

As I recall them, one by one, I feel like old King Midas. For they are all, all golden memories.

YOUR TRAVEL AGENCY BUSINESS CARD

Within a short time after you affiliate yourself with a travel agency, you will receive a business card identifying you as a member of the staff. The card will be printed with the agency's name, address, telephone number, and its corporate logo. If the agency is a member, the card may also have the insignia of A.S.T.A. (American Society of Travel Agents). Most important, it will have your name and title. This title could be Travel Representative, Sales Agent, Sales Representative, Travel Agent, Outside Sales, or the preferred Travel Consultant. Whatever you are called, this card, which recognizes you as a member of the travel trade, will open many new doors to you in the form of extraordinary discounts and courtesies within the travel and tourism industry. Here are some of the benefits you will receive:

Special Rates in Lodging

Many hotels and motels offer special discounts to the staffs of travel agencies. These discounts range from 10% to 75% of the walk-in or "rack" rate. In our experience, we have found that most participating hotels and motels extend a 50% discount to the travel agency staff.

Depending upon the frequency with which you use commercial lodging, this discount can mean to you hundreds, even thousands, of dollars in savings. There is a caveat, however, to pay heed to when using this privilege. Many hotels will only extend to you the travel agency discount if you call the sales office in advance (a day or two will suffice). Why? Because they want to make sure that space will be available and because they want to verify that, indeed, you are who you say you are—a bona fide Travel Consultant. Those leave-things-to-the-last-minute-type people who drop in at midnight, expecting a discounted room, might be sadly disappointed. Hotels only offer travel agency discounts if they expect to have a moderate to large vacancy factor. This is to be expected. The hotel/motel industry, of course, prefers to have their rooms occupied by guests who pay full price. Nevertheless, with proper planning and by avoiding travel at the busiest times, you should have little difficulty in finding excellent lodging at pre-inflation prices.

To better help you visualize how to go about utilizing this benefit, let me illustrate. Let's suppose that you are traveling to Chicago on business, where you have to stay for three nights. After deciding where you want to stay, call the hotel's sales office or front desk, identifying yourself as a travel agent. Ask what the rack rate is and if the hotel offers a travel agent's discount. Normally, if the walk-in rate is $70 per night, you will be quoted a rate of $35. Over the period of your three-day stay, your savings will amount to $35 × 3 days, which equals $105.

Not all lodging establishments participate in these discounts. Bed and breakfast inns do not, usually, offer price reductions. This is because they have a relatively small number of rooms to sell each night and thus, cannot be expected to extend such courtesies. There are times, especially during the off-season, when a discount may be offered at a bed and breakfast inn. If you do, indeed, have a strong desire to stay at one of the many charming inns

St. Moritz, Switzerland—A winter view of the world-famous Badrutt's Palace Hotel seen from lakeside—For skiers returning after a day on the snow-powdered slopes of the Alps, this fairy-tale scene represents good food, a warm drink, and a fire in the hearth by which they can unwind.

sprouting up throughout the country and you want to receive a discount, ask to speak with the owner or the manager. You might be pleasantly surprised to find him willing to accommodate your request.

Special Rates from Car Rental Agencies

With your travel agent's card, you will receive large industry discounts from car rental agencies. These discounts average 10% to 35%. All you need do, in most cases, is present your travel agent's card to receive an immediate discount.

Free Airport Parking

As you have probably realized, airport parking can be a great nuisance and a considerable expense. In some airports, parking costs as much as $10 per day. In the vicinity of most major airports, however, you will find hotels that offer free, unlimited parking to travel agency members. In most cases, all you have to do is present your card at the front desk and then leave another card on your car's dashboard so that it can be seen through the window. Your travel agency should be able to tell you which airport hotels in your area offer this much-appreciated service.

Reduced Entrance Fees

Your agency card will often qualify you for special discounts and free passes at many tourist attractions. Whether you are going to a museum or an amusement park, always go first to the administration office and present your card. When you are leading a group, you can almost always count on receiving a free pass. But even when you travel on your own, your card can be good for a discount or two.

The Travel Agency Card—don't leave home without it!

COMMISSION DEDUCTIONS ON PERSONAL TRAVEL

In the first chapter, I mentioned that many people believe there is a charge for the services of a travel agent. According to a recent survey, up to 67% of the public still clings to this erroneous belief. Instead, the travel agent's commission is built into the carrier's price. (A $500-plus-tax domestic airline ticket automatically includes a 10% commission to the travel agent.) Many agencies, as a courtesy to their staff members, have adopted the policy of deducting the full 10% commission on their personal travel. Perhaps a 10% savings does not sound like a lot, but when you consider that the average airline ticket costs hundreds of dollars, 10% becomes a significant sum. It can be likened to receiving one free flight ticket for every ten tickets purchased. In order to receive the full agency commission, you may need to fill out a special form provided by your agency. Because policies vary, do check with your agency.

FREE SEMINARS

Throughout the year, the travel industry takes its "dog and pony" shows on the road. Foreign governments, airlines, tour companies, cruise lines, and other industry suppliers journey to cities, large and small, to inform, entertain, charm, and "seduce" the travel agencies' personnel. They are there to sell their wonderful wares to the retail travel sellers. In these for-the-trade-only gatherings, you will learn a great deal. The seminar subject matter ranges from such topics as cruising the Amazon and exploring the Antarctic to the latest information on airline reservation systems. There are several advantages to be gained from attending these functions. They are:

Education

The information that you will acquire will enhance your expertise in your new field. A film about London, for example, narrated by a native, can transmit the same thrill (almost) as your visiting the city itself. This kind of exposure will enliven your presentations to your clients and thus increase your sales.

Networking

When you attend the seminars, make a point of meeting the suppliers' representatives. The more friends you make in the industry, the better job you will perform for your clients. Now, if and when there is a problem, you will be calling a friend at a supplier's headquarters, not a stranger. This can often make all the difference. Because you are no longer just a voice on the telephone, you just may receive preferential treatment. So don't be afraid to step forward and introduce yourself; seminars are not the place to be timid.

Fun and Enjoyment

All work and no play makes Jill a dull girl. Industry seminars are terrific places to meet your colleagues and make new friends. Many of these events begin with a social hour or a meal. This is a sure-fire way to create a convivial atmosphere. Most people in the travel business are fun-loving and casual, and that makes the seminars pleasant social occasions.

"FAM" TRIPS

Many hard-working and productive agents became involved in the tourist industry because of their desire to travel. One of the most wonderful vehicles for travel is the "fam" or familiarization trip. Fam trips are designed by cruise lines, airlines, tour companies, and tourist boards of individual countries in order to familiarize travel sellers with their cruises, flights, tour packages, and destinations. These familiarization trips often include your transportation costs, all meals, hotels, tours, and V.I.P. treatment, such as flowers and champagne in your room and on-site seminars at the destination. Different travel agencies have varying policies concerning fam trips. Some actually reimburse a portion of the cost of the trip to their most productive agents. However, if you are willing to pay for the fam trip yourself, the price of which is often as low as 20% to 50% of the normal cost, you should be able to go on several each year, if you so desire. Since you will be expected to attend seminars while on a trip of this nature, your reason for going should always be your genuine, professional desire to familiarize yourself with the destination. At this point, you might be wondering what kinds of fam trips are available. The following is a selective list of a few fams that were advertised in 1983 in *TravelAge West* magazine, a trade publication.

Copenhagen, Greece, Turkey—Love Holidays is offering a fam trip from Los Angeles to Copenhagen and on to Athens for a seven-day cruise of the Greek Islands and Turkey. Price of $591 includes land, air (via SAS) and cruise costs; two nights accommodations in Copenhagen; some meals; sightseeing; transfers; and taxes.

Ecuador and Galapagos—Unique Adventures and Eastern Airlines are offering agents a fam trip visiting Quito, Cuenca, Puyo, the Jaguar Jungle Lodge in the Rio Napo jungle, Ibarra, and Otavalo for $430 per person, double, including air. An eight-day Galapagos Islands extension, with a four-day cruise on the *Buccaneer*, is available for $465 per person.

Egypt—General Tours is offering 17 departures of a seven-day trip to Cairo, Aswan, and Luxor. Included in the price of $550 (single supplement $125) are accommodations, transportation within Egypt, some meals, sightseeing, guide, and transfers.

Alaska—Westours is offering 12 seven-day fam trips including Anchorage, river rafting, Columbia Glacier cruise, Valdez, Fairbanks, Denali National Park, and a wildlife tour. Cost of $325 per person, double, includes accommodations, receptions, some meals, and escort. Single supplement is $75.

Trans Siberian Express—Voyages of Discovery is offering a fam trip departing from either Los Angeles or Seattle via Finnair to Moscow, and passage on the Trans Siberian Express with a stop in Irkutsk. A visit to Leningrad is optional. The cost of $875 includes all air and train fares, hotels, meals, sightseeing, transfers, and an evening of theater in Moscow. The trip is $1,031 with the Leningrad visit.

Tahiti—Every week through 1983—Seven-day independent fam trips visiting Moorea, Bora Bora, and Papeete for $248 per person, double, and eleven-day trips that add Raiatea and Huahine for $312, per person, double, are offered by Specific Tours.

Scandinavia—General Tours is offering agents and spouses ten-day fam trips visiting Helsinki, Stockholm, and Copenhagen, with an overnight Baltic Sea cruise. Land cost is $550 to $595 for deluxe and superior accommodations. Land transportation, full breakfasts, some meals, sightseeing, transfers, and service charges are included.

This is just a sampling of the hundreds of fam trips offered each year. Gradually, as you become a more valuable member of your agency, you could qualify for the deluxe fams. For example, when the famed Concorde flight was inaugurated between the United States and London, some of the most productive agents from the larger agencies were the invited guests. And yes, they traveled gratis. If flying at Mach 2 is not your "speed," how would you like this? You are invited on a ten-day tour of Italy. You are flown first class, where you are pampered, served champagne, and fed mouth-watering delicacies. When you deplane at the Leonardo da Vinci Airport in Rome, a chauffeur-driven limousine awaits you to take you to your complementary suite at one of Rome's finest hotels... These kinds of trips are an example of the rarer "gems" among the fams, but they *can* be earned by *you* if you produce outstanding travel sales.

Cruise companies also have fam trips. In order to promote certain cruises, the major lines have promotional trips which are offered to travel agencies. If you are interested in going, your agency will put in a request with the company's representative. Your total cost for these cruises (which normally take place at the off or "shoulder" season) is usually an unbelievable $30 to $70 a day per person, with spouses welcome at the same rate! And yes, all cruises include room and all meals. The more cruise sales you and your agency create, the more you can expect to be invited on these floating dream trips.

As I mentioned previously, many agencies contribute financially to the low cost of these fam trips for their more productive agents. Elaine Lerner, owner of Group Travel Associates, reports that her agency chips in $75 per agent after they are employed for a year. That figure is increased to $125 from the second year on. Whether you are on the inside staff or in outside sales, expect to be rewarded for your productivity. Nevertheless, because

Maui, Hawaii—The Kapalua Bay Hotel is one of the finest resorts in the world. Here is a beginner's clue: You just can't go wrong booking group and individual travel in Kapalua.

their time is more flexible, outside sales people can often take advantage of more fam trips.

Familiarization trips add an incredible dimension to your travel career. For those who are willing to sell travel, the horizons are unlimited, and the skies are truly friendly.

PROMOTIONAL DISCOUNTS

In order to acquaint travel agents with their properties, hotels and resorts throughout the world advertise special rates and free stays. Since these promotions do not involve extensive seminars, they are not considered fam trips. Here is a small list of special sales and promotions offered by various members of the lodging industry. Again, these listings appeared in 1983 in *TravelAge West* magazine:

London and Paris—Sarova Hotels of London (Rembrandt, Mostyn, Rubens, and Washington) and Tradotel Hotels of Paris (Floride Etoile, Sydney Opera, Luxembourg, Beaugency, Eiffel-Hesperia, Eiffel-Passy, Montparnasse and Saint Germain) offer 50% off in a program called One-Two-Three Spree. Minimum stays of three nights in any of the above hotels cost $19 per person, double, per night; single rooms are $38. Agents' immediate families also qualify for the rate.

Hong Kong—The Regent Hotel is offering travel agents a 50% discount during the first period and a similar reduction during the Chinese New Year season.

Maui—The Maui Marriott Resort has extended its offer to accommodate agents free for three nights.

Mexico—Posada Vallarta Hotel and Village has a summer rate for agents of $12.50 per night, single or double.

Caribbean—International Travel and Resorts (ITR) is offering agents, and accompanying friends or clients, 50% off rack rates at seven of its hotels in Curacao, Barbados, and St. Thomas. Agents can get one room, if alone, or two rooms, when accompanied, at a discount for up to seven nights.

The promotional discounts do, indeed, bring new business to the establishments that provide them. In 1982, Nancy and I were invited by the Kapalua Bay Hotel in Maui, Hawaii, to stay as their guests at their lovely Bay Villas. Because we became enchanted with the property and were hosted so graciously by Michael Hu, the hotel's director of conventions and banquets, we brought a group of 130 people with us six months later.

THE 75 A.D. TICKET

Some of the most coveted travel benefits in the retail travel business are the discounted travel passes available through the A.T.C. (Air Traffic Conference) and I.A.T.A. (International Air Transport Association). Commonly called the 75 A.D. (agency discount) pass, this reduced-rate ticket offers a 75% discount on airline travel, both domestically and internationally. This is how the 75 A.D. pass works. Domestically, the Air Traffic Conference issues to an agency two passes for the first $100,000 in domestic sales it has produced. For each additional $100,000 in U.S. sales, the agency receives another pass. For example, if an agency does $1,400,000 annually (the national average, according to the Harris poll), it receives 15 passes.

I.A.T.A. issues its passes based on a different system. These passes, which are used for international travel, are issued at the rate of two for each travel-selling staff member who has been employed at the agency during the previous year for at least twelve consecutive months. In addition, recent new rulings permit a spouse to travel at a 50% discount, space available. On top of that, many airlines, as a result of the deregulation of the travel industry, offer free travel opportunities. One airline gave a medium-sized agency 400 free tickets just for installing its computer reservation system!

To illustrate the impact that a 75 A.D. ticket can have on your pocketbook, take a look at the following examples:

Round-Trip Ticket	Class	Regular Price (as of Nov. 1, 1983)	With 75 A.D. Pass
Los Angeles to New York	First	$1,300.00	$ 325.00
Chicago to Zurich	First	$3,238.00	$ 809.50
San Francisco to Miami	First	$1,126.00	$ 281.50
Seattle to Tokyo	Coach	$1,598.00	$ 399.50
Cincinnati to Honolulu	Coach	$1,238.00	$ 309.50
Atlanta to Frankfurt	Coach	$1,316.00	$ 329.00
Dallas to Jamaica	Coach	$ 546.00	$ 136.50
Washington to Tel Aviv	Coach	$2,074.00	$ 518.50
Toronto to Acapulco	First	$1,103.18	$ 275.80
Vancouver to Sydney	Coach	$3,428.00	$ 857.00
Philadelphia to Rome	First	$4,080.00	$1,020.00

As a Travel Consultant, you can qualify for a 75 A.D. pass. According to the *A.T.C. Travel Agents' Handbook,* section 15, to qualify, a person must be "an employee who is salaried and/or paid a commission and devotes full time (that is, not less than 35 hours per week) to the sale and promotion of transportation, including air transportation and related services." The Handbook also states that to qualify to be included on the reduced-rate list, one must not be otherwise gainfully employed. In practice, many travel agencies have interpreted this to mean that any Travel Consultant who earns commissions that are equivalent to the minimum wage × a 35-hour work week × 50 weeks is eligible to have his name on the A.T.C. and I.A.T.A. lists. Therefore, whether you generated those kinds of commissions for the agency by selling one high-volume group trip or by selling many individual trips is irrelevant to those agencies. I recommend that you find out, at the outset, what your agency's policy is regarding the 75 A.D. pass. Even if you cannot qualify for a 75 A.D. at this time, you can still benefit from free or reduced-fare travel. Your travel agency, especially if it does a large amount of business, can request from the carrier an occasional free or reduced-fare pass for its staff.

Are you as enthusiastic as I am about the travel opportunities and the marvelous benefits that are available to you as a Travel Consultant? Certainly, you will have to produce good results to enjoy them, but that is only right. There is no free lunch here—only the chance to reap exceptional financial and travel benefits for a job well done. As you become immersed in your profession, you will find yourself wanting to learn more and more about travel destinations, geography, and culture in order to better serve your clients. The travel amenities provided by the various members of the industry are designed to help you increase your expertise in selling travel. Learn and enjoy!

Bermuda—Fishermen congregate in Coot Pond inlet to prepare the day's catch. Peaceful scenes like this make Bermuda a charming, romantic place for clients looking to spend their first, second, or even third honeymoon.

I have just arrived back home from Europe with 850,000 other half-wits who think that a summer not spent among the decay and mortification of the Old World is a summer squandered.
WILL ROGERS

CHAPTER FIVE

GETTING STARTED

We have come a long way! Together, we have surveyed the various components of the travel industry as they apply to your career as a Travel Consultant. By now, you have learned a great deal about this extraordinary world. You have also discovered the wonderful opportunities awaiting you in the selling of travel. Perhaps you are dreaming of sandy white beaches, magnificent cathedrals, and roaring waterfalls. The world is your playground. Nothing can stop you now. And yet, at this very moment, I know that I am about to lose some of you. The reason I know this is because, in this chapter, I'm going to introduce what may be an uncomfortable word for many—WORK. Sooner or later, we must all face the fact that if we want to accomplish, we must act. Am I implying that you might be lazy? Not at all. I just know, through my years of experience in training and motivating many, that some capable individuals, when faced with a fine opportunity, do not take action. Like reluctant thoroughbreds, they never leave the opening gate. Why? I suppose it's because they are afraid. Afraid of what? Perhaps it's the fear of doing something they've never done before. Or, it might be the fear of being rejected—"Suppose nobody wants what I have to offer?"... "Will it work for me?"—that sort of thing. It is not within the scope of this book to offer a detailed analysis of human motivation and self-image psychology. Instead, may I challenge you? Whatever "demons" you have to contend with (and believe me, I have a few of these persistent "little devils" myself), I urge you to overcome them. You may not be able to rid yourself of them completely, but you *can* overcome them. It's really quite simple. Listen: **Action cures fear.** Say this to yourself out loud: "Action cures fear"... "Action cures fear." The beginning is always the hardest. But once you take those first stumbling little steps toward your goal, however hesitatingly, you're well on your way. There is much truth in that old saying that "getting started is half done."

In the following pages, I have outlined for you a detailed, step-by-step plan of action designed to help you get your Travel Consultant career off and running. Become thoroughly familiar with the contents. Study them until you're completely "at home" with this material. Naturally, life rarely follows a textbook. Nevertheless, this and the following chapter will teach you how to develop a solid foundation of good, repeat clients.

WILL THEY REALLY WANT ME?

Are you still wondering if a travel agency will be interested in your services as a Travel Consultant? While there are still agencies that do not have an outside sales staff, the trends clearly indicate that more and more agencies are relying on the take-the-business-to-the-customer method to increase their sales. The emergence of the Travel Consultant as a vital force is not limited to the United States. In the "Travel Industry Career" section of the August 25, 1983, issue of *Canadian Travel News,* twelve of the twenty-five "help wanted" ads were for outside sales Travel Consultants! In these ads, three of the travel agencies promised to provide in-house training for their new Travel Consultants. To further illustrate how valuable you can be, here is a small sample of "help wanted" ads which appeared recently in *TravelAge West,* the respected travel industry magazine owned by Dun and Bradstreet:

WELCOME OUTSIDE AGENTS—Attractive Saratoga location; split commissions; many benefits; management open to negotiations; please call ...

OUTSIDE SALES—Commercial travel agency needs Outside Sales Reps with following or potential; generous commissions; scale plus bonus incentive; terms negotiable; send resumé. . .

OUTSIDE SALES—Earn high commissions; automated in Beverly Hills area; call now ...

IF YOU ARE AN OUTSIDE SALES AGENT, are you completely happy with your agency? If the answer is yes, tell your employer so and continue to do a good job. If the answer is no, we may have a better alternative for you. Call ...

In addition to the reasons outlined in the first chapter, a growing number of travel agency owners/managers are eager to employ productive Travel Consultants because of the economics involved. Unlike the inside staff, who, as employees, are paid a salary and receive employee benefits regardless of their productivity, Travel Consultants, most of whom are self-employed as independent contractors, are only paid when the travel agency receives a commission as a result of their efforts. In addition to the question of productivity, Travel Consultants take very little of the travel agency's limited space. In contrast to inside staff members, who need one desk each to do their work, good Travel Consultants spend the bulk of their time in the field developing new accounts and servicing their clients. Because of this, one desk area can comfortably service eight or more outside sales people. All of this can spell lower overhead and higher profits to the travel agency owner. It also means that your profession represents an important force within the travel business. Because you are willing to take the business to your clients instead of waiting for your clients to come to you, you are creating new outlets and opening up previously untapped markets for your travel agency and the industry at large.

YOUR HIDDEN ASSETS

Are you still plagued with doubt? Perhaps your mind is responding with new, more personal objections, such as, "I don't know anyone," or "I just can't sell," or "I don't have enough education." Don't let the old excuses hold you back any longer. For example, if you genuinely feel that you don't know anyone, perhaps because you're new in town, simply make a point of meeting new people. There are hundreds of worthy organizations, from sports clubs to volunteer groups, that are crying for new members. Also, don't be afraid to say "Hi." Most people, whether at the supermarket or in church, will respond in kind. (If someone does not say "Hello" back, you don't have a prospect!) A simple greeting can lead to a conversation in which you are asked, "And what do *you* do?" As you can see, excuses are not real problems; they are just convenient alibis. (A friend once defined the word, "excuse," as "the skin of a lie stuffed with a reason.") A productive life consists of challenging problems solved by creative answers. If you adopt this kind of problem/solution philosophy toward your new profession, you will enjoy an exciting and successful career.

It is now time to take an inventory of your assets. You will need to convince two different people of your abilities to succeed in the travel business—you and a travel agency owner. Unless you can visualize yourself as a productive member of the world of travel, nothing will happen. Next, you must convince a travel agency owner of your value to his agency's future. You will accomplish this through an effectively written resumé and through a personal interview. In order to help you take stock of your many hidden assets, the following questionnaire was prepared. Before reading further, **right now**, why don't you get a notebook and a pen and answer these questions in detail. Your answers should give you the confidence to proceed with your new career and offer a foundation for an impressive resumé. Do not concern yourself with answering each question in the affirmative; they were designed to include a large cross-section of personality types and experiences.

Your Hidden Assets Questionnaire

1. Do you have any sales experience? Before answering "no," think—have you ever sold Girl Scout cookies, delivered newspapers, sold Avon, or helped in a fund drive?

2. Do you belong now or have belonged in the past to any organizations? (a church, a club, a sports' organization, a veteran's group, a bridge club, a bowling league, a business group, P.T.A., a homeowner's association, etc.)

3. Do you have a large family? Are you part of a

supportive family group who would buy travel from you?

4. Do you have lots of friends?

5. Have you ever done any volunteer work?

6. Have you done any travel?

7. Are you an organized person?

8. Do you set goals and then work to achieve them?

9. Do you belong to an ethnic group?

10. Are you a self-motivated individual?

11. Can you grasp details quickly?

12. Do you have a pleasant personality?

13. Are you willing to meet with group or corporate officers to sell them your services?

14. Do you have an unusual desire to succeed?

15. Are you persistent?

16. Do you enjoy public speaking?

17. Do you like to organize people?

18. Do you enjoy feeling useful and needed?

19. Will you work for recognition?

20. Do you have any special talents, interests, areas of expertise, or job experience that can be utilized in the travel business?

Even if you answered "no" to most of these questions, you can still be successful in travel. While your past connections and experiences can, indeed, prove to be an asset to you, *by far* the most important factor is your determination to succeed. Remember this: Success comes to those who turn their stumbling blocks into stepping stones.

HOW TO CHOOSE A TRAVEL AGENCY

Having taken stock of your individual assets and having examined your value as a Travel Consultant, you are now ready to choose a travel agency with which to be affiliated. Selecting the right agency is an important ingredient in your success recipe, and with over 23,000 agencies to choose from in the U.S. alone, it is not an easy task. To get the most from your meetings with the various travel agents, you must develop the proper posture toward your interviews. If you go to your interviews "on your knees, hat in hand," hoping that someone will give you a break, you are just *not* going to be very impressive. No one wants to associate with a person who has a "victim" mentality. Instead, develop the attitude that you are going to be a tremendous asset to the travel agency—in a sense, causing the owner to wonder, just a little, how he ever got along without you. When you select an agency to interview, find out as much as possible about it, its owner, and its specialty. Most metropolitan areas have annual travel shows in which many agencies are represented. At these gatherings, you can find out quite a bit about each agency by asking questions of the staff members. In addition to these general rules, here are a few specific tips on selecting the right travel agency for you:

1. **Avoid new or very small agencies.** With some notable exceptions, new agencies have less experienced personnel. Since you are learning a new trade, you're better off working with the most experienced (and patient) people you can find. Small-volume agencies qualify for fewer travel benefits. And that can mean limited travel opportunities for you. Also, as mentioned earlier, larger agencies, by reaching specific sales volumes, can receive additional commission bonuses from the airlines, cruise lines, and tour companies, which they often share with their sales staff.

Courtesy: Sitmar Cruises

St. Thomas in the U.S. Virgin Islands is a popular port-of-call for many cruise ships. Passengers love to browse the duty-free shops of Charlotte Amalie, the island's capitol. In this photo, Sitmar Cruises' *Fairwind* awaits the return of its bargain-hunting passengers after a day of colorful shopping.

2. Choose an agency with a successful outside sales program. While many enlightened agencies actively court good outside sales people, some still run their operations without Travel Consultants. In your search for the right agency, seek out only those that have an enthusiastic attitude about an outside sales program. Prior to visiting various agencies, make some telephone calls. Ask each one you call if they employ outside sales people. If they respond with a "no" answer, they may not be right for you. By making appointments with only those agencies that have ongoing sales programs, you will save much time and effort.

3. Interview the owner or manager. It is important that you see the owner or the manager of the travel agency in person. Tell him that you are eager to start a part-time or full-time career as a Travel Consultant. Since you have taken inventory of your assets, list those assets to the owner, and give him your resumé. If he expresses interest in you, ask the following questions:

a) "Do you have, **in writing,** a program that outlines the commission splits with Travel Consultants?"

b) "Do you have, **in writing,** a breakdown of agency-covered and personal expenses?" Make sure that you know which expenses you are responsible for and which expenses are covered by the agency. For example, you will probably be responsible for the office phone calls you make to clients and tour companies. The travel agent will probably pay for the computer time and cost of issuing tickets. To avoid surprises, find out the policy of the agency before you get started.

c) "Will I be welcome to attend all staff meetings?" Make sure that you will be given all the considerations of the inside staff. This way, you will be able to continue to learn and to grow in your new field.

d) "Will I have a contact person inside the agency who will help me 'learn the ropes'?" It's important to have a "buddy" on the inside staff. Be sure to ask for one.

e) "Do you have a contract for me to sign as an independent contractor?" Make sure that everything is spelled out exactly. Being an independent contractor has many benefits, which shall be covered later on.

4. **Interview the inside staff.** If you feel positive about your interview with the agency owner, take time to meet the staff members. Make sure they also have a good attitude about outside sales people. Tell them that you hope your additional production will be an asset to the agency. If you encounter any hostility, look elsewhere. Remember, because you have the potential of bringing new business to any agency, you are in the "cat-bird seat!"

5. **Interview the agency's existing outside sales staff.** Ask to speak with the top producers. If the agency has a good outside sales program, the owner should be glad to give you their names. Why do I recommend that you speak with only the most successful Travel Consultants? Because I already know what the non-productive ones will offer you—excuses, excuses, and more excuses. Always associate with winners if you want to be one. They have been "through the ropes," but they are not "on the ropes." They can give you a realistic appraisal of their experiences with the agency. In addition, you can gain a great deal of practical knowledge from their travel-selling expertise. If the agency has a star performer, by all means, ask that person to become your mentor and teach you the "rules of the game."

THE INDEPENDENT CONTRACTOR STATUS

One of the advantages to be gained from becoming a Travel Consultant is the qualification for the status of independent contractor. An independent contractor is any person who is not an employee who is contracted to perform a service at an agreed-upon price. What are the advantages of being an independent contractor?

1. As an independent contractor, you have tremendous flexibility. You are your own boss! You can do as much or as little business on any particular day as you feel like doing. By law, an independent contractor cannot be told when to work and which meetings to attend.

2. As a self-employed person, you can start your own retirement program. If you wish, you can even incorporate your business.

3. No taxes will be withheld from your income by the travel agency.

4. All business-related expenses will be deductible. Without giving any legal advice, self-employed people can deduct all expenses related to business, such as home office deductions, car expenses, travel expenses, expenses associated with entertaining clients, self-employed retirement programs, expenses associated with further education, books and magazine subscriptions related to your business, telephone expenses, the employment of a family member to help with paperwork, and much more. Please check with your tax advisor for his recommendations.

Recently, in an attempt to lure the most productive and experienced Travel Consultants to their staffs, particularly those with group and commercial accounts, some travel agencies have been offering a guaranteed salary plus commission to experienced outside sales professionals. Whether this kind of arrangement is best for you or not is a decision you will have to make for yourself. If you feel more comfortable as an employee and prefer a guaranteed salary, you might welcome the security of a salary base, even if it means lower commissions. If, however, you are more entrepreneurial and enjoy maximum commissions and complete freedom, the independent contractor status will suit you best.

TO SPECIALIZE OR NOT TO SPECIALIZE

Deciding what type of outside sales career you want is another question that you should resolve. You can either specialize in one or two areas of travel, or you can choose to serve clients with all their travel needs. As of right now, if you have relatively little knowledge of travel but you do have a broad circle of friends and associates, it might benefit you to service them with their complete travel needs. At a later date, as you become more knowledgeable about the various facets of travel, you may choose to handle the one area that appeals to you most. If you are interested in developing more profit earlier, you may want to immediately start calling on businesses and associations and having them book their travel through you and your travel agency. In this case, as a new Travel Consultant, you will probably act as a finder. Once you create a new commercial account, you will need to enlist your agency's help with the proper details. (See chapter seven for an in-depth discussion of group and corporate travel.) Some people may choose to specialize right away in one area. I know a Lisbon-born travel agent who does most of his business with Portuguese people in northern California. He understands their language and their needs, and as a result of specializing, he has prospered.

One advantage that you have as a Travel Consultant is that you can focus exclusively on an area of personal interest to you. (A travel agent, in contrast, must book all destinations and handle all carriers and, therefore, cannot specialize fully.) One couple who is interested in hiking has developed a business of organizing backpacking trips in the Alps, the Himalayas, the Andes, and the Rocky Mountains. They have combined their hobby with a lucrative travel business. Today, they have their own wholesale tour operator company specializing in worldwide hiking trips.

As you can see, the opportunities are endless. Success in business is defined as "finding a need and filling it." As a Travel Consultant, you have the opportunity to find your very own niche in the endless mosaic of travel opportunities.

Cruises—A Profitable Specialty

If you choose to specialize but you do not have ethnic connections or unusual interests, a good area in which to focus your efforts is in the sale of cruises. The reasons why cruises are an excellent specialty are:

1. Cruise lines offer larger commissions. They usually pay 12% to 15% versus 8% to 10% by the airlines. In addition, if you work with a high-volume, cruise-oriented travel agency, you may receive bonuses and free cruises, as described earlier.

2. Cruises offer complete vacations. Once your client is on the ship, he is provided with all his needs, and, as a result, you have no more details to worry about. This makes the travel arrangements relatively hassle-free. Therefore, a new Travel Consultant with little experience may find cruises an ideal way to get started.

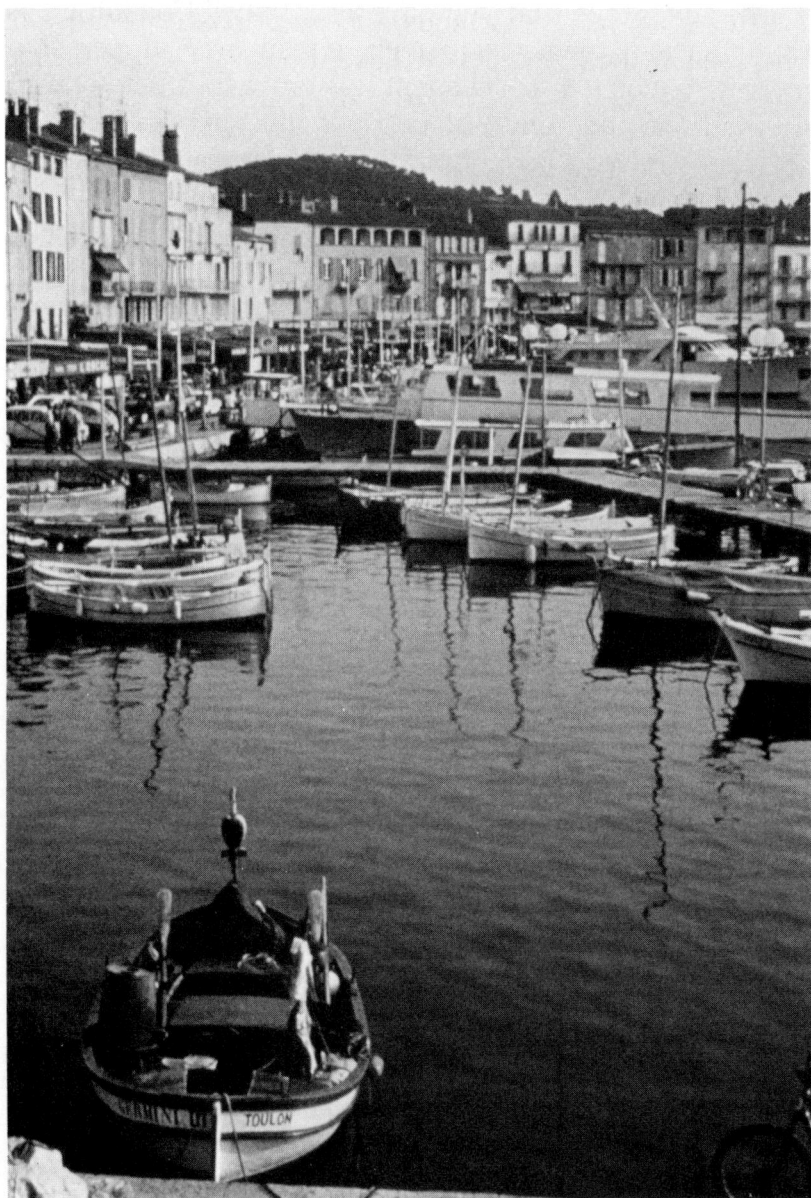

The French Riviera conjures images of the idle rich in string-thin bathing suits browning themselves langorously along the Mediterranean, under the lazy noon sun. But to the fishermen of St. Tropez, the sea represents their daily struggle with the fickle Poseidon to bring in the bounty he yields so reluctantly.

3. Cruises have enormous appeal. Partially because of the television show, "The Love Boat," cruises, which used to appeal mostly to the affluent elderly, are now attracting enthusiasts from every segment of the population. One type of client who has been grossly neglected, in my opinion, is the blue collar worker. As cruises become more affordable and as blue collar workers' income has begun to equal and even exceed that of many office workers, there is a huge untapped market of willing clients who simply have not been approached by anyone.

Another widely neglected area for selling cruises (and travel, in general) is our ever-expanding population of affluent Blacks and Hispanics. One must search high and low to find advertisements that address themselves to this extremely important market. What a shame! These high achievers, who have overcome more than the normal share of obstacles to reach their elevated station in life, are generally flattered when their success is recognized. Your soliciting them as clients is a form of recognition of their achievement. Because of this, you should enjoy excellent response in this emerging market.

In spite of all the interest shown in cruises recently, only 5% of the population has ever experienced one. And yet, I would bet that almost everyone would thrill at the idea of taking a cruise. Without a doubt, your potential for profits is high in cruise sales.

HOW TO MAKE A PROSPECT LIST

You have already taken stock of your inner assets: your talents, your skills, and your potential. Now the time has come for you to uncover another form of hidden assets by making an exhaustive list of the people you have known throughout the years. It is all too easy to skip over the task of composing a written list of prospective clients. I would venture to say that most of the people in travel sales have not taken the time to complete this essential step. And yet, your prospect list is your gold mine. Your first clients will probably emerge from this valuable source. How much time should you devote to this vital project? As much time as it takes, but two hours would not be unreasonable. I can't stress enough the importance of developing your list **in writing**. Why? Because the human mind does not recall more than a few names at a time. As a matter of fact, why don't you do yourself a favor and get a special notebook for your prospect list. Carry it with you at all times. This way, whenever a name comes to mind, you can immediately write it down. Many people draw a blank when they attempt to think of who they know. They interpret this failure to remember as an indication that they don't know enough people to succeed. Invariably, the opposite is true. Through the years, their minds have stored the names and impressions of *so* many individuals that they suffer from sensory overload. One of the best techniques to overcome this temporary forgetfulness is to use the "who do you know" method as a memory jogger. By categorizing the various groups of people that you know, you can start a veritable snowball of names. The following questionnaire is designed to help you compile your prospect list:

The "Who Do You Know" Questionnaire

1. Who is on your holiday/Christmas list?

2. Who do you know because of your children, your spouse, or your parents?

3. Who do you know because of your job or your former job?

4. Who do you know because of sports activities?

5. Who do you know because of church activities?

6. Who do you know because of service club activities?

7. Who do you know who does a lot of travel?

8. Who do you know who has talked of taking a vacation this year?

9. What groups do you know that would enjoy taking a vacation together?

10. Do you have ten or fifteen friends or business associates who might be interested in taking a trip together? Who are they?

11. Do you belong to any business groups that would enjoy going on a tax deductible trip/seminar? Which group?

12. Do you know the president of any social club?

13. Who do you know from high school or college? (Get out your old annuals.)

14. Who do you know who are neighbors or former neighbors?

15. Who do you rent from?

16. Who sold you your home?

17. Who sold you your car?

18. Who do you know who is a physician, a dentist, an attorney, a veterinarian, a chiropractor, a pharmacist, an optometrist, a nurse, or an accountant?

19. Who works in a bank?

20. Who owns a store in your area or performs a service for you? (dry cleaners, plumber, florist, printer, hairdresser, or car mechanic)

21. Who do you know who serves the community?

(school board, fire department, police department, clergy, or volunteers)

22. Who has a job that requires a great deal of plane travel?

23. Who goes to a national convention at least once a year?

24. Who do you know who is retired?

25. Who has an important birthday or anniversary coming up?

26. Who do you know who has children attending a school in another state?

27. Who do you know who has relatives living overseas or in a different section of the country?

In addition to this questionnaire, here are two more methods to help you expand your list:

1. **Use the yellow pages.** Go through the yellow pages of your telephone book from A to Z. Look at each heading, and take note of the various occupations (from accountant to zoo keeper). Do any of these professions "ring a bell?" You just might remember the interior decorator that you met at the school picnic last year or the friendly computer programmer you used to commute with.

2. **Get out your membership rosters.** Do you belong to an organization that has a membership roster? What about the symphony league? the high school staff? your church? a civic club? the Chamber of Commerce? If you don't know the members personally, you can always send them a letter to explain your services. Later, you can follow up in person.

These ideas and guidelines should give you an excellent basis for a prospect list. By all means, use your imagination and creativity. You will be amazed to discover how many more names you will think of.

WHY YOUR CLIENTS
WILL BUY FROM YOU

It's only normal that a client will want to know why he should buy his travel tickets from you rather than from the airlines or from a travel agency directly. The answer to this question lies in the kind of service that you're willing to provide for customers. **Only if you give outstanding service can you expect to have a loyal following.** With this in mind, here are some reasons why a client should prefer to work with you:

1. **You will research the best fares.** Today, more and more travel agencies are being computerized, with most of the computer systems having been designed by such airlines as United, American, and Delta. What the public does not realize is that most of the computer systems are biased in favor of the airline that designed them. Furthermore, charter flights, which usually offer good values, may not be represented on the computer at all. By subscribing to travel magazines and by keeping up to date, you can find the best rates available for your clients and thus save them money.

2. **You will offer custom-tailored service.** With their large overhead, travel agencies must generate a great deal of business every day just to pay their bills. As a result, their often-harried inside staff members can show impatience with the rudimentary questions of the less-experienced traveler. Also, many travel agents do not acquire a detailed profile of their clients' travel habits and interests (see Appendix). You, as a Travel Consultant working primarily out of your home, with little overhead, can afford to groom your clients with more care than they would most likely receive at many travel agencies. With

today's kaleidescope of travel options, this kind of hand-holding treatment is the only way that many neophytes will venture forth and begin to travel.

3. **"We make house calls."** Let's suppose that you have a client who wishes to plan a vacation for his family. You can visit your customer at his home or office, work within the family budget, and write down all the pertinent information. Once you have planned the trip and taken care of the reservations to your client's satisfaction, you can deliver the tickets personally. Can you afford to do this? Let's say that you help a friend plan an Hawaiian vacation for his family of five. The total price of the tickets, hotel, and car rental comes to $4,000. Even if you take five hours to work on this trip, it would still be worth your while. The agency's commission will be approximately $400. If you, as a Travel Consultant, receive a 40% commission, you will make a profit of $160, or about $32 an hour. For this amount of money, would you be willing to "make house calls?"

*Of journeying the benefits are many: the freshness it
bringeth to the heart, the seeing and hearing of marvelous
things, the delight of beholding new cities, the meeting of
unknown friends, the learning of high manners.*
SADI

CHAPTER SIX

PROMOTE! PROMOTE! PROMOTE!

TWELVE GREAT WAYS TO DEVELOP CLIENTS

Even if you build a better mousetrap, the world will *not* beat a path to your door. Today's consumers are lazy. They must be reminded constantly that you are there to serve them. Conclusion? Get the word out to everyone that you can do a better job of taking care of their travel needs.

Listed below are twelve ways by which you can develop an unlimited number of clients. While not all of these methods may fit your particular personality, at least one or two definitely will. The most important thing to do is choose one of these techniques and get started.

1. **Direct contact**—Did you compose a thorough list of prospects? If you haven't, do it now! It's okay, I'll wait for you......Ready? Now, call the people on your list. Tell them that you are starting a new career in travel and that you would like to explain to them how they can save money and receive better service from you. Emphasize to them that your services will not cost them any additional money. Immediately ask for an appointment. Make sure that both of you record the date and time of the appointment in your calendars. As soon as you schedule the appointment, **get off the phone.** Remember this money-making rule: Never attempt to sell over the telephone if you can visit your prospects in person. Why? Because the phone is one-tenth as effective as a personal visit.

2. **A general-announcement letter**—In addition to the people that you know well enough to call, you can reach others by circulating a general-announcement letter in your area. This letter should explain your service and inform the recipient that you will be calling them for an appointment. One way to develop a mailing list is to consult a reverse directory. This valuable book gives the names of individuals living on a particular street (with house numbers) and can be found in your local public library. The reverse directory can allow you to target specific neighborhoods. Once you have mailed your letter, follow up by calling within a short period of time. Remember, ask for the appointment without trying to explain further your services over the telephone.

There is a variation to your sending a general-announcement letter. If you're a bit more ambitious, you can include in each letter a questionnaire which consists of travel-related questions, such as: Are you taking a vacation this year?—Does anyone in the family travel on business?—Do you currently work with a travel agent? You can have fun making up your own survey. If you print a short list of questions on a postage-paid post card (you can arrange this with your local postmaster), you will make it easy for people to return your survey. Naturally, those who answer your questionnaire and mail it back are prime prospects.

3. **Referrals**—Whenever you visit with a potential client, ask for referrals. Referrals are your "ticket" to an endless supply of names. Those who ask for them are increasing their chances for greater success. This is what to do. At the end of your initial appointment with a client, ask, "By the way, Linda, who do you know who would also enjoy this kind of personalized travel service?" If Linda is cooperative, ask her if she would mind calling three or four of her friends, while you're still there, to recommend that they set up an appointment with you. You will be surprised to find out how many people will want to help you, so don't be afraid to ask. By asking Linda for assistance, you're getting her involved in your enthusiasm. You're also creating a growing network of new clients.

4. **Travel parties**—This method of developing clients has to be the biggest "sleeper" in the travel industry. Have you ever been to a party-plan presentation, such as Tupperware or Sarah Coventry? If you have ever attended one of these kinds of gatherings, you have a rough idea of how they work. The formula is simple: invite a few friends, play a few games for entertainment, demonstrate the products, and take orders. This is how you, as a Travel Consultant, can use the party plan concept to book vacation travel and find new customers:

a) Meet with the owner of your travel agency and inform him that you want to develop a travel party plan. Explain to him that you will be needing some gift items for the hosts and guests and that you would like his help. If the owner is reluctant, stress to him that each party will constitute free advertising for the travel agency. Such items as travel bags, luggage tags, pens, sunglasses, and ash trays—all with the agency's logo—are most suitable. From time to time, many cruise companies, airlines, and hotels offer discounts. You may want to include these among the prizes. (After all, they cost the travel agency nothing.)

b) Next, find couples or singles who will act as hosts. You're most likely to find willing candidates from among your current clients.

c) Help the hosts make a list of prospective guests. (Refer to the "Who Do You Know" list for ideas.) If the hosts belong to any groups with a common affinity (bowling league, church, singles' club, etc.), have them invite those people, as well.

d) Prior to the travel party, discuss with the hosts the type of travel program most suitable for their friends. It is essential that you target your travel presentation to your audience. For example, a white-water rafting trip through the Grand Canyon may not be suitable for a group of octogenarians. Once you have determined the best kind of vacation for the group, ask your travel agent to help you locate the most suitable slide show or movie on the subject.

e) Have your hosts invite their friends by saying, "A friend of ours, (your name), is a Travel Consultant. He's going to show a terrific travel film/slide show in our home. I expect it to be a wonderful evening. I'd like you [both of them, if a couple] to come. Because of limited space, I need to know if you can definitely make it—may I count on you?"

One of the biggest problems in party plans is the "no-show" factor. Therefore, if you want to have ten couples at the presentation, have your hosts invite twice as many. Make sure they encourage both husband and wife to come. This is important because you want people to be able to make buying decisions on the spot. Naturally, you will have to give your hosts an incentive for holding the party. This incentive can be based on the number of trips sold as a result of the party. Your travel agent might even entice a nearby resort to donate one night's free lodging in return for the free promotion. If the hosts belong to a group that would go on a trip together, you can offer a volume discount to everyone based on the size of the group. With enough people going, the hosts could even earn a free trip.

Travel parties—another great way for you to develop a lucrative travel business!

5. **Circulate**—One of the best ways for you to create new contacts is to circulate in your community. By becoming active in various civic projects and clubs, you will be able to meet many new people and tell them about your business. Here, let me add a word of caution. Make sure you affiliate yourself only with projects in which you have a genuine interest. Otherwise, you will not enjoy yourself, and people will question the reason for your involvement. Always, "to thine own self be true."

6. **Business cards**—Give your business cards to everyone you meet, including sales clerks. (You can even attach your business card to bill payments.) If you have a travel specialty, make sure that it is printed on your card. Have your Travel Consultant "hat" on at all times, even when you're doing your household shopping or going to the cleaners.

7. **Seminars and lectures**—Some people find it a bit difficult to sell their services aggressively. A less direct but not-less-effective way to promote yourself is to give seminars and lectures. There are many topics from which to choose. One subject that is of interest to almost everyone is "how to save money on travel." There are abundant opportunities for you to speak in front of the public. Service organizations, such as the Lion's Club and the Junior League, thirst for fresh, new speakers. In

addition, many schools have an adult education program which they offer to the community. If you are willing to plan a short course on travel and the school is interested in your topic, you may even be paid a fee for being the instructor. When you teach a course or give a lecture, you become an expert in the minds of your listeners. A subtle (or not-so-subtle) mention of your travel service can lead to new clients for you.

8. **Write a column**—In your area, no doubt, there is a neighborhood throw-away bulletin or a community newspaper. You can contact the editor and volunteer to write a column on travel-related topics. Your by-line, enhanced by your smiling portrait, will establish you as a travel "personality" and will give you free publicity in your community.

9. **Brochures**—Collect all the travel brochures that you can. Your travel agent should be delighted to give them to you. Stamp your name and address on each one of the brochures, and place them in such locations as hospitals, doctors' offices, dentists' offices, and beauty salons. It's a good idea to staple your business card to each one of the brochures. This is another way to keep your name in front of the public.

10. **Advertise**—As a self-employed business person, you are free to advertise. I recently discovered a quarter-page ad in the yellow pages of the San Francisco telephone book that was promoting the services of a Travel Consultant. (The ad proclaims, "We make house calls," and does not have an agency's name attached to it.) As your business grows, you may want to develop an advertising campaign. I caution you to be conservative, however, in spending money on lots of advertising. As you are getting started, it may be an unwise expense.

11. **Newsletters**—By the time you have twenty-five or more clients, you may want to start writing your own newsletters. Sent out monthly, newsletters keep your

Yes, Virginia, this is New York. Far from the madding crowd there is a little island of tranquility called the Mayfair Regent Hotel, where every afternoon tasty little sandwiches, delicate pastries, and steaming hot tea and coffee are served in the palatial surroundings of the lobby/lounge. For your most discriminating clients.

name in front of your clients on a regular basis and create good will. In addition, you can use your newsletter as an effective advertising tool. How? There are a couple of ways you can accomplish this. In each issue, you can ask your clients to mention your services to their friends. You can also set aside several copies of your newsletter to be sent out to prospective clients and prominent business people in your area. Your newsletter can be fun and interesting without being either long or fancy. One typewritten page announcing discount fares and new travel opportunities is sufficient.

12. **Agency mailing list**—Put your clients' names on your travel agency's mailing list. Arrange, however, to have your name appear on all the literature that your customers receive. This way, you can benefit from your agency's promotional efforts.

As you can see, you have an endless supply of potential clients. Although writing newsletters and having your customers' names on your agency's mailing list will not primarily help you in developing new clients, these methods will increase your likelihood for consistent travel sales.

THE APPOINTMENT

Good for you! You have now contacted one of your prospects who has agreed to set an appointment with you. Now, what do you do? Before you succumb to the onrush of vertigo and heart palpitations, relax! It's all quite simple. Your prospect is not an adversary, but a friend. You have much good news to offer, so smile. One key to your success is to be prepared. Here are some "tools of the trade" that can help you greatly:

The Presentation Book

Prepare a presentation folder that outlines all of the services and benefits that you have to offer. For ideas, refer to the section in the previous chapter, "Why Your Clients Will Buy from You." By pasting pictures and brochure headlines throughout, you can give your folder an up-beat, exciting look. Instead of doing this at random, however, target your presentation. For example, you can cut up brochures and advertisements in such a way as to have a page or two on each of the most popular destinations. A presentation book which highlights the Caribbean, Hawaii, Mexico, a popular cruise, and a

London theater package is likely to serve as an effective introduction to travel. Obviously, if your clientele is geared toward a particular destination (such as Israel or Japan) or consists of sophisticated travelers, design your presentation folder accordingly. By all means, be creative! Put the stamp of your unique personality into this and all other projects.

Some Travel Consultants actually assemble several travel folders so that they can leave a copy overnight with a client. This is an excellent idea because it gives your prospect the opportunity to "sell himself" on the idea of taking a trip. It also gives you a reason to come back within a few days to pick up your folder and to follow up on your prospect's travel interest.

The Questionnaire

Another important item to include in your initial presentation is a questionnaire. Your goal in having your prospect answer a list of questions is two-fold:

1. You need to qualify your prospect. Too many sales people try to "tango" with people who "don't want to dance." Your prospect may not have any plans to travel anywhere in the next twenty years. What should you do? Leave him alone! He does not qualify. Politely leave, drive home, and as you enter your front door, make a "Carson-esque" motion of teeing off with your golf club as you yell, "Next!" By asking the right questions, you can find out very quickly about the "travel-ability" of your prospect.

2. If your customer is qualified, the questionnaire will give you a profile of his travel needs. This will allow you to gear your presentation to his particular areas of interest. What kinds of questions should you include in your survey? Perhaps your travel agency has already compiled a list of questions. If not, here are a few good examples:

- Are you planning to visit any family members this year? If so, will this trip involve the use of any public transportation, such as air or train travel? How about hotels and car rental?

- Does either of you travel on business extensively? If so, how often?

- Are you going on any group trips or conventions? If so, where and when?

- Are you planning any vacations this year? If so, where and when?

- If you haven't yet planned a vacation, would you be interested in taking one if it could fit into your budget?

- Have you ever been on a cruise? Would you like to go on one?

- If money were no object, where would you travel?

- What do you prefer in a vacation—adventure and excitement or sunny beaches and relaxation?

At each appointment, have a customer card on which you note the answers to these questions. You may also want to record the birthdays and anniversaries of your prospect's family. Aside from the courtesy of sending a card, what could be a more romantic anniversary present than a week's cruise in the Caribbean or a getaway weekend at a nearby resort? For more ideas, take the time to study the traveler's survey prepared by Jeanne Gay, publisher and owner of the Travel and Tourism Press. (See Appendix.)

Unlike other types of sales, the primary goal of your initial appointment is *not* to have your customers sign on the dotted line. Instead, it is to establish yourself as their Travel Consultant. Just as the C.P.A. is hired to take care of tax matters, you are the professional who helps your clients with their travel needs.

According to the Simmons Market Research consumer study, most Americans would rather spend their discretionary income on travel than on remodeling their homes or on buying new cars. Armed with this knowledge, you should have an easy time developing an eager group of travel-hungry clients. So have fun with your appointments. After all, you are bringing the magic and glamour of travel to your prospects' lives. What could be more welcome?

FOLLOW-UP

When your clients return from their trips, call them to welcome them back home and to inquire about their impressions of their vacations. Note their comments on your customer cards. This information will give you clues as to what your clients enjoy and what future vacations you should propose to them. For example, if they just came back from Ocho Rios, Jamaica, and loved their trip, send them a brochure of a similar Caribbean location with a note, saying, "I think you will really enjoy this as your next destination."

As you can see, by sending a brochure, you are already preparing your clients for the next trip—a wise move. There is a saying about the difference between a good pool player and a great pool player: A good pool player focuses on getting the ball in the pocket; a great pool player does the same thing, but in addition, he makes sure that he has positioned himself for the next shot. By learning and employing the techniques of follow-up, you, like the great pool player, are positioning yourself for greater success as a Travel Consultant.

THE TEN COMMANDMENTS
OF HUMAN RELATIONS

An anonymous sage compiled a list of the Ten Commandments of Human Relations. As a fitting conclusion to this chapter, I would like to present them to you:

1. Speak to people. There is nothing as nice as a cheerful word of greeting.

2. Smile at people. It takes 72 muscles to frown, only 14 to smile.

3. Call people by name. The sweetest music to anyone's ears is the sound of his own name.

4. Be friendly and helpful. If you would have friends, be a friend.

5. Be cordial. Speak and act as if everything you do is a genuine pleasure.

6. Be genuinely interested in people. You can like almost everybody if you try.

7. Be generous with praise. Be cautious with criticism.

8. Be considerate with the feelings of others. There are usually three sides to a controversy—your side, the other person's side, and the right side.

9. Be alert to give service. What counts most in life is what we do for others.

10. Add to this a good sense of humor, a big dose of patience, and a dash of humility, and you will be rewarded many-fold.

If you can live up to all of these commandments every day, they will put the title of "Saint" in front of your name. Nevertheless, these are worthy goals for which all of us can strive.

Aside from advertising to the public, the travel industry wholesalers spend large sums to woo the retail travel agent. Here, in this lovely ad, the Austrian National Tourist Office quietly sings the praises of the *gemütlich* (roughly translated as "relaxed charm") character of the land and its people.

The soul of a journey is liberty, perfect liberty, to think, feel, do just as one pleases. We go a journey chiefly to be free of all impediments and of all inconveniences; to leave ourselves behind, much more to get rid of others.
WILLIAM HAZLITT

CHAPTER SEVEN

GROUP AND CORPORATE TRAVEL— THE "BIG TIME"

How hungry are you? Would you be content to make good extra income by serving individual clients with their travel needs, or are you interested in making a fortune? Both options are open to you in outside sales. The choice is yours. In order to make a *great deal* of money, you need to employ the concept of time leverage. What is time leverage? Simply put, if it takes you one hour to develop a new individual account, it would take 50 hours to develop 50 new individual accounts. But if you have 50 people as part of a group going to the same destination at the same time and it takes you one hour to develop that account, you are leveraging your efforts by getting 50 times more business for the same hour of work. Even if it requires twice as much time to develop your group account, you are still multiplying your results and earnings by 25 times. Herein lies the advantage of selling group travel.

Another way of leveraging your time is by developing corporate or business accounts. If you can land an exclusive account for your travel agency with a business that books 10 flights per month, you have multiplied your effectiveness many times over. With 10 flights per month, you have generated for your agency 120 bookings per year. At a $500-average transaction, you have helped to create $60,000 in business for your agency.

Corporate and group travel is Big Business. According to the Travel and Tourism Government Affairs Council, in 1981, business travel accounted for 64% of all hotel industry revenues and 56% of all passenger miles flown on U.S. airlines. According to American Express, in 1982, American companies spent over 70 billion dollars on travel, with the growth of business travel having outpaced the inflation rate.

GROUP TRAVEL SALES— AN UNTAPPED GOLD MINE

One of the most exciting statistics in the travel industry is that only 10% to 15% of all associations and groups currently use a travel agency to handle their present convention business. Moreover, there are literally thousands of business groups, trade associations, service clubs, and professional organizations that would gladly organize an annual trip if only someone would approach them with a proposal. In my own experience, as the head of a large direct-selling organization, I have never been approached by a travel agency with a proposal to develop a trip or to organize a travel seminar. It was only when Nancy and I saw the motivational value of such events that we affiliated ourselves with a travel agency and started organizing our own trips. If you are willing to be creative and to research the many different types of organizations in your area, you could develop a lucrative group business. To enable you to do a good job, make sure that you align yourself with a travel agency that has the experience and professionalism to provide you with the proper support. Unfortunately, this kind of agency is not easy to find; therefore, be selective.

One of the reasons that associations and group members like to travel together is psychological. Most of us prefer traveling with people we know. When our environment changes, as it does in travel, it's a comfort to have familiar faces around us. Many people prefer traveling with their peers. Physicians, for example, are more at ease traveling with other doctors (probably because they are less likely to be asked for free medical advice). In addition, if the trip is designed as a seminar and complies with the Internal Revenue Service's rules for professional/educational travel, part or all of the cost of the trip can be a tax-deductible expense (a great selling point!).

Twelve Steps to Develop a Group Travel Program

In a recent seminar on selling cruise travel, Richard Revnes, the innovative and aggressive president of Royal Cruise Lines, addressed his audience on the tremendous potential in group travel. He made the following suggestions on how to go about organizing a trip for organizations. I have amplified his excellent recommendations with my own extensive experience in dealing with the promotion of trips for business groups. The following twelve steps should help to ensure your success in developing group travel:

1. **Target the "core" of the group.** All organizations have essentially the same dynamics. An organization is made up of a diverse group of people who share at least one area of common interest. Of this group, about 10% will make up the core of loyal, committed, and active

members. The rest range from inactive to moderately active in their involvement with the organization. Expect 75% to 80% of your passengers to come from this core of active members. Focus most of your promotion on this nucleus of "believers."

2. **Contact the right person in the organization.** Because his programs are already set, the current president is not your best contact. Instead, sell your group travel proposal to the incoming president. Call him and explain that you have a proposal that will help him better retain the current membership as well as create new members. Avoid explaining your proposal over the telephone. Remember, only use the phone to set an appointment.

3. **Make it easy on the incoming president.** Most association presidents are volunteers who have little time to devote to their office. Therefore, at your appointment, assure the incoming president that your travel plan will involve no risk, no work, and no obligation on his part. Instead, ask his permission to allow you to promote the trip within the organization. Mention, in a subtle, off-hand way, that if there are enough people participating, it is customary for the president and spouse to act as hosts on the trip and to have their travel expenses paid.

4. **Choose a popular trip.** In selecting the right package for a group, concentrate on a destination or cruise that will have a universal appeal to the members. For the first trip, don't get too exotic—stay with the popular destinations (no camel caravans across the Sahara or balloon flights over the North Pole).

5. **Be sensitive to the makeup and goals of the group.** If you are approaching a country club, for example, choose a destination with first-class golf facilities. Sometimes, the choice is not so obvious. Your local pediatric association, for instance, will be made up of members with a more diverse background and more

varied interests. In this case, a luxury cruise may be a safer choice.

6. **The more information you have about an organization, the better.** If you know a member of the group you are approaching, ask him some questions about the organization. Find out about its history, the likes and dislikes of the members, and the special terms and titles that are used in the group. There is nothing more complimentary to members of an organization than to receive acknowledgment and respect from an outside person. The more you understand the needs and aspirations of the group, the better job you can do to serve its members.

7. **Advertise and promote.** You can advertise and promote your trip in several ways—by mail, by phone, by holding a membership meeting, or with a combination of all three methods. The larger the group, the more it becomes worth your while to employ a combination of ways to make the desired impact. It's advisable to hold a meeting only if a large number of the members can get there within a 25-to-30-minute time frame.

8. **Choose a convenient time.** If you have decided to hold a promotional meeting, it's best to hold it mid-week—on a Tuesday, Wednesday, or Thursday evening—ideally at 7:30 or 8:00 p.m. Since you are selling a "dream," pick a meeting place that is nice enough to enhance your message. Proper air conditioning, comfortable seating, and good lighting are all important. Make sure that the sound system is adequate and that you know how to use it. You may want to decorate the room with posters, flyers, and props representing the destination you are selling. Another good idea is to play recorded music that evokes the trip, such as French songs played on an accordion, Hawaiian guitar music, the sounds of a mariachi band, or the rhythms of a calypso combo.

9. **Ensure good attendance.** The most important ingredient in having a successful meeting is to have people show up. Many beginners neglect the essential detail of ensuring good attendance. In order to catch the attention of the members, you must remind them of the meeting in several ways. **Only multiple reminders will create enough attendance to ensure the success of your trip.** Here are three successful ways to promote the meeting:

a) Write an article that is signed by the president for inclusion in the upcoming issue of the association newsletter. The article should announce a special meeting to discuss "a new and exciting travel program." Make sure that both husband and wife are invited and are urged to come together.

b) Follow up the general announcement with a personalized invitation, again, signed by the president. Include a telephone number so that the members can call in to make a reservation. Because of the limited amount of seating, ask for a confirmation (R.S.V.P.). Don't count on the president to write the invitation. Have an effective promotional piece written. You can either write it yourself, or you can elicit the help of your agency's staff. All the president has to do is approve the invitation letter and sign it.

c) Telephone all the members two days before the meeting, saying, "I'm calling on behalf of President _____, who is looking forward to seeing you at the meeting. Can he count on you and your spouse to attend?"

10. **The small details count.** In addition to the pre-meeting preparations recommended in item #8, at the night of the meeting, you can further improve your odds of selling your trip by paying close attention to the following details:

a) Have the president greet the members at the door and introduce you to them in positive, warm terms. The introduction could be something like, "I would like to introduce you to my friend, (your name), who has a presentation that I know will be of interest to all of us here tonight."

b) Have name tags available for everyone. This will make it easier for you to call the members by name.

c) Avoid alcoholic drinks at the beginning of the meeting. But do serve coffee, tea, and punch. A cup in hand is a great "security blanket" for the Linus in all of us. It helps everyone relax.

d) Have background music playing. It helps to create a party atmosphere.

e) Circulate before the meeting and socialize with people. By asking them questions about themselves, you will create a friendly and trusting audience. Don't try to sell the trip yet.

f) Show a good film on the trip destination. The following suggestion might seem elementary, but make sure that you know how to operate the equipment and that the projector, the screen, and the movie are in good working order. Don't leave that to chance!

g) If you have brochures of the destination, pass them out to your audience. Go over them from the stage, and highlight those areas that you think will be of particular interest to your listeners. When describing travel destinations, use as many descriptive adjectives as possible, such as "sun-drenched" beaches, "palatial" accommodations, "mouth-watering" salads, "endless" sunsets, and "sumptuous" buffet feasts. (Get the picture?) To balance this suggestion, don't get too carried away by stretching the truth. If the group is going to spend a few days in a budget hotel in London, do not describe the facility as if it were Claridge's. Therefore, make sure that your travel or cruise deserves the accolades you give it, or you just might have disgruntled clients on your hands a few months hence.

h) After your presentation, have the host get up and ask how many people have an interest in the trip. At this point, I like to pass out a questionnaire. This questionnaire simply asks for the person's name, address, and phone number. It contains only one statement: "I would like to go on the trip to (location)," or "I would like to go on the cruise." I then give a choice of one of three boxes to check:

☐ Yes, definitely.

☐ Maybe.

☐ No.

This kind of sheet will allow you to follow up properly with each of your prospects by letter or by phone.

i) Have a table set up near the exit to take deposits. "Early bird" special incentives work very well. You may be able to offer a discount or premium gift, such as a flight bag, to those who register that night.

11. **Use direct mail.** In developing your direct-mail campaign, I recommend the following steps:

a) Send your mailings to those who attended the meeting as well as to those who were unable to be there. When you compose the letter, make sure you cover all the important points once again.

b) If your budget allows it, send out a color brochure. Do not spend too much money on this, however. I have found this item to be a much less important factor than the *right* price and the *right* destination.

c) Instead of writing the direct-mail piece on your agency's letterhead, have the letter printed on the organization's letterhead and signed in blue ink by the president. In the letter, have the president state: "We are going. I want you to go. It's going to be great fun to travel together." The more personal the letter, the better.

d) It sometimes works better to send the letter to the wife rather than to "Mr. and Mrs." Certainly, send all mail to the home address and not to the office.

e) If you feel that you have not yet earned the complete trust of the group, have the checks written to the organization or to the president. It is quite simple to arrange for the checks to be endorsed over to your agency.

12. **Follow up personally.** In addition to the mail piece, personally call all of the people who marked the boxes on the questionnaire with a "Yes, definitely" or a "Maybe" reply. Those who checked the "Maybe" box *really* want to go, but they may have a personal challenge to overcome, such as the fear of flying, a financial hurdle, or a reluctant spouse. A caring phone call or even a personal visit can induce another person to go on your trip.

According to Richard Revnes, fewer than 10% of the organizations in any area have been approached by a travel agent or consultant. Your potential in this untapped market is endless. It is entirely possible for you to develop a full-time career by concentrating on groups and associations and by learning to cater to their travel needs.

CORPORATE TRAVEL SALES—
THE WAY TO RESIDUAL INCOME

Everyone would like to have I.B.M., Amway, General Motors, or U.S. Steel as a corporate account. Visions of millions of dollars in annual commissions, bringing instant wealth, flash through the minds of the starry-eyed travel agent and Travel Consultant. My advice to you concerning these accounts is simple—forget them! That's right, I said, "Forget them!" You are probably confused and slightly outraged. You could be saying right now, "How can you, Ben, be so negative and fatalistic after encouraging me to think big and to overcome my fears? Aren't you the hypocrite?" Actually, I want you to be successful. In business, to be successful, you have to find a need and fill it. The big corporations in America are inundated with sales pitches from the large travel organizations, such as American Express and E.F. MacDonald. You simply cannot compete on this level at this point in your career. However, the good news is that while everyone wants to land the big accounts, there are hundreds of thousands of potential small businesses which employ from 2 to 150 people whose accounts remain unsolicited. This is where you can find your gold mine.

As a Travel Consultant, your role in developing commercial accounts is not to sell your services. Instead, your job is to convince the company to use the services of your travel agency. Corporate clients need fast, efficient, and automated services and will deal with the reservation staff of the agency directly. Perhaps this analogy will help. In the Sacramento First National Bank, where I am a founding director, we have business-development executives. These valuable people talk to potential clients and bring in new accounts. But once those accounts are developed, the actual daily business transactions are handled by the inside staff of clerks, cashiers, and loan officers.

Once you have developed a new business account for your agency, you can be compensated in several ways. Because there is no standard way of handling your compensation, you have every right to negotiate an agreement with your travel agency. Make sure that your agreement is in the form of a written contract. To quote one of Samuel Goldwyn's malapropisms, "A verbal contract is not worth the paper it's written on." So protect yourself! One of the simplest and fairest ways to compensate a Travel Consultant for developing new corporate accounts is this. For each corporate account, the Travel Consultant will receive 1% of the net commission the first year and ½% commission from the second to the fifth year, as long as he is actively affiliated with the travel agency. For this commission, the Travel Consultant will be expected to maintain good will with the business account and to help with any problem that might arise. How much money can you earn for bringing in one account? Lynne Sorensen, one of the most successful outside sales Travel Consultants, reported recently that she spent one day developing a good corporate account for a travel agency. That account proceeded to spend $600,000 that year on travel. At 1% commission, Lynne earned several thousand dollars for one day's work.

Because you will be selling the services of your travel agency when you call on business accounts, you should develop a well-defined marketing presentation that emphasizes the strengths of the agency. This plan should be worked out with the agency's management/marketing staff. Once you have a marketing presentation, start by targeting your efforts to establishments with which you have done business. As a customer, you will have the ear of the business owner. As you start calling on businesses with relatively small travel needs, you will be able to practice your presentation in more friendly surroundings.

Many of these small business people will be complimented by your desire to have them as customers. Always ask for several referrals. One commercial account can lead to several others. Whenever possible, have your new customer call two or three of his colleagues on the phone to recommend your service. As you can see, by using this method, your travel business can experience a "'snowball" effect.

Have you ever heard a success story that did not include a few setbacks? Of course not! The same is true with your career in travel. On your road to success, you, too, will have some setbacks and will encounter rejection along the way. Not every business owner will be receptive to your proposal. There may even be days when it will seem to you that nothing you do is working. (I know.) Consider this, however: Unless you experience "noes," you will not profit from the "yeses." There are no "days" without "nights." That's the way it is. The good news? Because there are so many people and organizations that need your service, you, through pleasant persistence, can develop an exciting and lucrative career.

★ ★ ★ ★ ★

As we reach the end of our "journey" together, I am satisfied that I have fulfilled my promise to you—to show you how you can start and succeed in your own Travel Consultant business. The travel business will provide you with endless opportunities for success. Many experts predict that by the year 2000, travel will become the largest industry in the world. As you have now learned, most of that market is still untapped. Now, the ball is in your court. Will you act? I sincerely hope so. Whether this is the right business opportunity for you or not, I hope that this book has sufficiently inspired you to join those who have become active participants in our free enterprise system.

Courtesy: Sitmar Cruises

Bon Voyage!

AFTERTHOUGHTS...

If There Are No Travel Agencies Where You Live

In spite of the tremendous growth in the number of travel agencies throughout the United States and Canada, there are still thousands of small towns, villages, and thinly inhabited areas that cannot support the services of a full-fledged travel agency. If you live in such an area, consider yourself fortunate. As a Travel Consultant, you can become the travel professional where you live. To do so, contact a travel agency and offer to represent it in your community. Although you may prefer it, it is no longer necessary to represent an agency from a neighboring town or city. Today, there are large travel agencies that are recruiting outside sales personnel on a nation-wide basis. Some agencies are even providing their Travel Consultants with an "800" toll-free number for calling in their customers' reservations. Also, as the role of computers increases, Travel Consultants will be able to communicate with their agencies via computer modems attached to their telephones.

M.I.T.A.

Until recently, the only nation-wide support groups for travel agents provided membership exclusively to the travel agency owner or to the highly experienced agency professional. The American Society of Travel Agents (A.S.T.A.) and the Association of Retail Travel Agents (A.R.T.A.) gear their valuable services primarily to the travel agency owner. The Institute of Certified Travel Agents (I.C.T.A.) focuses on the accreditation of travel agents who have at least five years' experience. As a result of this limited representation, only about 20% of the

127

more than 150,000 members of the retail travel industry have been able to belong to a national support group.

In 1982, Bill Stephan, a young and enterprising travel agent, founded M.I.T.A., an acronym for Membership for Individual Travel Agents. In a recent telephone conversation, Bill described his organization as a "professional service membership organization in support of individual travel agents." Membership in M.I.T.A. is open to all agency staff members who sell travel at least thirty hours a week. This includes new and part-time agents and Travel Consultants. According to Bill, M.I.T.A. benefits include:

- a bi-monthly newsletter
- a "gold" card identifying the holder as an agent
- exclusive fam trips for M.I.T.A. members
- counseling service for agents
- employment information
- special travel benefits
- group health insurance.

In its first year of operation, M.I.T.A. has attracted over 5,000 members. Should you have an interest in joining and supporting M.I.T.A., write or call:

M.I.T.A.
27895 Narciso, Dept. TD
Mission Viejo, CA 92692
Telephone: (714) 831-6225

APPENDIX

APPENDIX

Appendix I

CONTRACTS AND AGREEMENTS

Alexander Anolik, the best-known travel-law attorney, advises each year on the buying, selling, appraising, and setting up of hundreds of travel agencies throughout the country. His advice to outside sales Travel Consultants is to have a fair contract between themselves and a travel agency. Such a contract, which spells out the rights and obligations of both parties, will minimize confusion and will, therefore, aid in the formation of a long-term, mutually beneficial relationship.

A full explanation of the legal differences between the independent contractor and the employee, as well as additional travel law information, is available in his *Preventive Legal Care* tapes-and-syllabus album set and in his book, *The Law and The Travel Industry*. (These items can be obtained from Alexander Anolik, a Professional Law Corporation; 693 Sutter Street, Sixth Floor; San Francisco, California, 94102; or from Travelstrength; 885 Sunset Drive; San Carlos, California, 94070. The price for the *Preventive Legal Care* tape series is $75.00; the price for *The Law and The Travel Industry*, which includes a supplement, is $29.95.)

The following is Alexander Anolik's Outside Sales Agent Contract for the independent contractor. This sample contract is dated November, 1983.

EMPLOYMENT CONTRACT
OUTSIDE SALESPERSON/INDEPENDENT CONTRACTOR

PREFACE

[It should be understood that the designation above of an Outside Salesperson as an "Independent Contractor" in an employment contract will not protect a travel agency from liability for the failure to withhold income taxes, the obligation to pay Unemployment Compensation, or for a negligent act of the Outside Salesperson. The determination of such liability is based upon a number of additional factors, including the degree of control the travel agency exercises over the activities of the Outside Salesperson/Independent Contractor. The word "retains" may be substituted for "employs" in a contract to emphasize the Agent's lack of direct control over such activities of the salesperson.]

AGREEMENT made this _____ day of _____ 198___, between _____(Name of Travel Agency)_____ , a travel agency, having its principal place of business at _____(Address)_____ , hereinafter referred to as the Travel Agency and _____ _____ , of _____(Residence Address)_____ , _____(City)_____ , _____(State)_____ , hereinafter referred to as the Independent Contractor.

FIRST

TERM OF AGREEMENT

The Travel Agency hereby retains the Independent Contractor and the Independent Contractor hereby accepts such retention with the Travel Agency for a period of _____ _____ beginning on the _____ day of _____ , 198___; however, this Agreement may be terminated earlier as hereinafter provided.

SECOND

DUTIES OF INDEPENDENT CONTRACTOR

The Independent Contractor is employed and retained by the Travel Agency to sell travel and travel services to the public on behalf of the Travel Agency.

The Independent Contractor at all times during the performance of this contract shall strictly adhere to and obey all the rules and regulations regarding the scope of employment of outside sales representatives as promulgated by the Air Traffic Conference and the International Air Transport Association governing the conduct of employees as now established, or as subsequently modified by the Travel Agency in accordance with applicable conference resolutions and any state and/or federal law.

THIRD

COMPENSATION OF INDEPENDENT CONTRACTOR

Expenses

Independent Contractor shall be reimbursed by Employer for "technical assistance" expenses (items such as badges, luggage tags, document holders, envelopes and postage to mail documents) and approved promotional expenses incurred in connection with sales made by the Independent Contractor. Said reimbursement shall be made on the last day of each month during the term of this Agreement.

As compensation for the services rendered by him under this Agreement, the Independent Contractor shall be entitled to commissions on sales as follows:

Commissions

Gross Profits: The Independent Contractor shall be entitled to _____ percent (_____ %) of the Gross Profits realized by the Employer for retail sales of travel or services. Gross Profits shall be defined as commissions on sales rendered to the Employer less directly attributable expenses, including but not limited to, costs of tour guides, tour expenses, telephone charges and brochures. Override commissions rendered to the Employer for volume sales shall not be considered a part of the Gross Profits.

Commercial Accounts: The Independent Contractor shall be entitled to the following commissions for referrals of Commercial Accounts:

Net Commission to Employer of:	Independent Contractor is Entitled to:
Up to $ _____ per month	_____% of the Net Commission
Between $ _____ per month and $_____ per month	$ _____ plus _____ % Net Commission exceeding $ _____
Between $ _____ per month and $_____ per month	$ _____ plus _____ % Net Commission exceeding $ _____
Over $_____ per month	$ _____ plus _____ % of the Net Commission exceeding $ _____

The net Commission is defined as the Commission to the Employer minus any gifts (i.e., flowers, tote bags, Christmas gifts, etc.).

Additional Compensation

The Independent Contractor shall be entitled to the following additional compensation:

a. After ninety (90) days from the signing of this contract or the retail sale of $ _____ of travel services: Hotel and car discounts as specified by the Travel Agency;

b. After one hundred and eighty (180) days from the signing of this Contract or the retail sale of $_____ of travel or services: a personal trip for employee and spouse for a trip not to exceed a retail value of $ _____;

c. After the retail sale of $ _____ of travel or services: available land package deductions as specified by Travel Agency.

FOURTH

EXAMINATION OF BOOKS

The Independent Contractor shall have the right, either personally or by an accountant retained and paid by the Independent Contractor, at times mutually convenient to the Travel Agency and the Independent Contractor, but in any event at least once during each half of the calendar year, to examine books and accounts of the Travel Agency insofar as they relate to transactions affecting the amount of the Independent Contractor's compensation.

FIFTH

OBLIGATIONS OF INDEPENDENT CONTRACTOR

The Independent Contractor will not, at any time, either himself/herself or through others, solicit or divert, or attempt to solicit or divert, clients, customers, sales or business from the Travel Agency to, or for, any other travel agency, or anyone, either while still employed or following the termination of this employment, for a period of __ (   ) years within the following county/counties:

_____ .

The Independent Contractor will not, at any time, either himself/herself, or through, or with the aid or assistance of others, take, misappropriate, or misuse any client list, name, file, book, record or account or other information or confidential data used at or in the Travel Agency business.

SIXTH

TERMINATION OF EMPLOYMENT

Events Causing Termination

The Agreement shall terminate immediately on the occurrence of any one (1) of the following events:

a.   The occurrence of circumstances that makes it impossible or impracticable for the business of the Travel Agency to continue;

b.   The death of the Independent Contractor;

c.   The willful breach of duty by the Independent Contractor in the course of his performance of duties unless waived by the Travel Agency;

d.   The habitual neglect by the Independent Contractor of his/her duties, unless waived by the Travel Agency;

e.   The continued incapacity on the part of the Independent Contractor to perform his/her duties, unless waived by the Travel Agency.

Effect of Termination on Compensation

In the event of the termination of this Agreement prior to the completion of the term of employment specified herein, the Independent Contractor shall be entitled to the compensation earned by him/her prior to the date of termination as

136

provided for in this Agreement computed *pro rata* up to and including that date; the Independent Contractor shall be entitled to no further compensation as of the date of termination.

Time Limit For Claiming Commissions
After Date of Termination

All claims of the Independent Contractor for commission on sales, regardless of whether the sales are made by the Independent Contractor or others, are waived by the Independent Contractor if not made within sixty (60) days of the date of termination.

SEVENTH

Remedies

Any controversy or claim arising out of, or relating to, this Agreement, or the making, performance, or interpretation thereof, shall be settled by arbitration in __(Name of City and State)__ _____ in accordance with the rules of the American Arbitration Association then existing, and judgment on the arbitration award may be entered in any court having jurisdiction over the subject matter of the controversy.

Attorneys' Fees and Costs

If any action at law or in equity is necessary to enforce or interpret the terms of this Agreement, the prevailing party shall be entitled to reasonable attorneys' fees, costs, and necessary disbursements in addition to any other relief to which he may be entitled.

EIGHTH

GENERAL PROVISION

Partial Validity

If any provision of this Agreement is held by a court of competent jurisdiction to be invalid, void or unenforceable, the remaining provisions shall nevertheless continue in full force without being impaired or invalidated in any manner.

Law Governing Agreement

This Agreement shall be governed by and construed in accordance with the laws of the (State)_____ .

Executed at _____ , (State) _____ , on the day and year first above written.

AGENCY NAME

By: _____
(name and title)

INDEPENDENT CONTRACTOR

By: _____

[The preceding Employment Contract-Outside Salesperson/Independent Contractor has been prepared as an example only. It does not constitute legal or professional advice. Anyone intending to use this contract should modify the language or substitute other provisions where, as will always be the case, varying circumstances require. It is suggested that every Agent or individual contact his or her travel attorney to determine what particular or additional contract provisions apply.]

CLIENT-PREFERENCE SURVEY

The following survey was created and used by Jeanne Gay, one of the foremost experts on cultural tourism today. Jeanne is also the author of *Travel and Tourism Bibliography and Resource Handbook,* a definitive opus in three volumes (1,328 pages). It is an indispensible guide to any serious student of travel and tourism. To order your copy, send $50 to:

> Travel & Tourism Press
> P.O. Box 1696
> Chico, CA 95927

TRAVELER'S SURVEY & CLIENT CUSTOMIZING PROFILE

We would like to know all about your travel and tourism likes and dislikes in order to provide you with information, books, materials, and bibliographies to enrich your tourism experience. It will also allow us to suggest and/or secure travel and tourism arrangements whose components match YOUR needs and desires.

NAME: _____

ADDRESS: _____

PHONE NUMBER: (Home) _____ (Office) _____

AGE BRACKET: 18-29_____ 30-45_____ 46-60_____ Over

60_____

WHERE HAVE YOU TRAVELED BEFORE?

☐ East U.S.A.	☐ Central America	☐ Africa
☐ West U.S.A.	☐ South America	☐ Middle East
☐ Alaska	☐ British Isles	☐ Asia
☐ Hawaii	☐ Europe	☐ Orient
☐ Canada	☐ Iberia	☐ South Pacific
☐ Caribbean	☐ Scandinavia	☐ Polar Regions
☐ Mexico	☐ Eastern Europe	☐ Round-the-World

WHICH AREAS DID YOU PARTICULARLY ENJOY? _____
_____

WHICH AREAS WOULD YOU LIKE TO GO TO THAT YOU HAVEN'T
SEEN BEFORE? _____
_____

WHEN DO YOU USUALLY TAKE YOUR VACATION?

Winter ☐   Spring ☐   Summer ☐   Fall ☐   Flexible ☐
WHAT LENGTH OF TIME DO YOU USUALLY HAVE AVAILABLE FOR
VACATIONING? PLEASE GIVE APPROXIMATE NUMBER OF:
Weeks ☐   Months ☐   Varies ☐   Unlimited ☐
WITH WHOM DO YOU USUALLY TRAVEL?
Alone ☐   Spouse ☐   Spouse & Children ☐   Friend ☐   Varies ☐
IF YOU TRAVEL WITH YOUR CHILDREN, PLEASE INDICATE SEX AND
AGE OF EACH:
_____
_____

HOW DO YOU PREFER TO TRAVEL?

- ☐ With individual travel arrangements
- ☐ On a package tour
- ☐ On an organized tour with escort
- ☐ Variety of ways, depending on area
- ☐ Other: _____

HOW DO YOU LIKE TO TRAVEL?

- ☐ Air: First Class ☐ Economy ☐ Charter ☐
- ☐ Car: Own ☐ Rental ☐ Chauffeured ☐ RV ☐
- ☐ Rail: First Class ☐ Coach ☐ Railpass ☐
- ☐ Motorcoach: Large ☐ Medium ☐ Small ☐ Van ☐
- ☐ Ship: Liner ☐ Cruiser ☐ Freighter

DO YOU ENJOY A TRIP INVOLVING A COMBINATION OF TYPES OF TRANSPORTATION? _____

DO YOU HAVE A PREFERRED AIRLINE? _____

DO YOU PREFER A WINDOW, CENTER, OR AISLE SEAT? _____

SMOKING OR NON-SMOKING SECTION? _____

DO YOU HAVE A PREFERENCE IN CAR RENTAL FIRMS? _____

WHAT SIZE/TYPE OF CAR DO YOU USUALLY RENT? _____

WHAT SIZE OF SHIP DO YOU PREFER TO SAIL ON?

Large ☐ Medium ☐ Small ☐ Yacht ☐ Schooner/Yawl ☐

WHERE DO YOU PREFER YOUR CABIN TO BE LOCATED?

Midship ☐ Forward ☐ Aft (rear) ☐

Upper deck ☐ Middle deck ☐ Lower deck ☐

DO YOU HAVE A PREFERRED SHIPLINE AND/OR SHIP?

_____

_____

WHAT TYPE OF HOTELS DO YOU PREFER?

- ☐ Ultra modern
- ☐ Traditional
- ☐ Inns/Pubs
- ☐ Motels
- ☐ Pensions/Bed & Breakfast
- ☐ Castles/villas
- ☐ Resorts
- ☐ Ranches/farms
- ☐ Variety of types
- Other: _____

WHAT CLASS OF HOTELS DO YOU PREFER?

☐ Deluxe ☐ Tourist

☐ First Class ☐ Budget

☐ Moderate ☐ Variety, depending on area

PREFERENCE IN SIZE AND LOCATION OF HOTELS:

☐ Large, multi-convenienced

☐ Medium, traditional conveniences

☐ Small, personal service

☐ Tiny, very personal

☐ High rise bldg. ☐ Low rise bldg. ☐ One floor

☐ City center ☐ Suburb ☐ Country, scenic

☐ Seaside or lakeside ☐ Desert ☐ Mountains

☐ Variety, as marked above. Other:_____

PREFERENCE IN HOTEL ACCOMMODATIONS:

☐ Suite ☐ Single room ☐ Room/standard double bed

☐ Room/queen double bed ☐ Room/king double bed

☐ Room/two double beds ☐ Room/twin beds

☐ Triple room ☐ Quadruple room ☐ Dormitory

☐ All rooms with private bath: ☐ Tub ☐ Shower

☐ Private facilities not essential

☐ Other needs or comments:_____

_____

PREFERENCE IN HOTEL FACILITIES DESIRED:

☐ Garden setting ☐ Shops/boutiques

☐ Historical significance ☐ Gourmet dining

☐ Interesting architecture ☐ Fine wine cellar

☐ Swimming pool ☐ Floor show

☐ On beach or lake ☐ Casino/gambling

☐ Tennis courts ☐ Jacuzzi/sauna

☐ Golf course ☐ Jogging path

☐ Horseback riding ☐ Bicycling

Other: _____

_____

142

HAVE YOU EVER BEEN ON A FULLY STRUCTURED TOUR? (i.e., all-inclusive group itinerary with a tour escort)

Yes ☐   No ☐

IF YES, WHO WAS THE TOUR OPERATOR? (i.e., American Express, Cartan, Brendan, etc.)

_____

DID YOU ENJOY IT?_____

IF NOT, WHY? _____

IF YOU WERE OFFERED A STRUCTURED TOUR THAT MET ALL OR MOST OF YOUR SPECIFICATIONS, WOULD YOU TAKE IT?

_____

WHEN YOU ARE TOURING, HOW MUCH SIGHTSEEING DO YOU ENJOY?

Maximum ☐   Moderate ☐   Minimum ☐

WHAT TYPE OF SIGHTSEEING DO YOU ENJOY?

In depth ☐   Highlight ☐   Historical ☐   Modern ☐

Museums ☐   Cathedrals/churches ☐   Castles/palaces ☐

Cemeteries ☐   Scenic views ☐   Gardens ☐   Zoos ☐

Other: _____

_____

_____

_____

PLEASE INDICATE ANY SPECIAL INTERESTS YOU HAVE THAT YOU MIGHT LIKE TO HAVE INCLUDED IN YOUR TRAVEL ARRANGEMENTS:

☐ Genealogy	☐ Cultural events
☐ Gardens/forests	☐ Theater performances
☐ Photography	☐ Musical performances
☐ Architecture	☐ Sports events
☐ Antiques	☐ Gambling
☐ Walks/hikes	☐ Special events
☐ Vineyards/wine tasting	☐ Folklore
☐ Gourmet restaurants	☐ Thematic history
☐ Cooking classes	☐ Archaeology
☐ Bicycling	☐ Anthropology
☐ Fishing	☐ Religious
☐ Hunting	☐ Environment-ecology
☐ Golfing	☐ Fine arts
☐ Tennis	☐ Hand crafts
☐ Skiing	☐ Shelling & beachcombing
☐ Sailing	☐ Exploring caves
☐ River rafting	☐ Scuba diving

DO YOU REQUIRE A SPECIAL DIET? (i.e., salt-free, vegetarian, kosher, etc.)

_____

_____

DO YOU HAVE A HEALTH OR HANDICAP PROBLEM THAT SHOULD BE ACCOMMODATED IN YOUR TRAVEL & TOURISM ARRANGMENTS?

_____

_____

YOUR COMMENTS/THOUGHTS ARE MOST WELCOME:

_____

_____

PLEASE RETURN YOUR COMPLETED PROFILE TO:

Thank you!

144

Appendix III

GEOGRAPHIC DISTRIBUTION OF TRAVEL AGENCIES

BY STATE AND PROVINCE

A.T.C. COUNT OF U.S. AGENCIES BY STATE
(as of September 30, 1983)

Alabama 103
Alaska 88
Arizona 340
Arkansas 65
California 4,109
Colorado 451
Connecticut 523
Delaware 44
District of Columbia 187
Florida 1,552
Georgia 304
Hawaii 271
Idaho 58
Illinois 1,296
Indiana 272
Iowa 166
Kansas 144

```
Kentucky .......................................... 111
Louisiana ......................................... 191
Maine ............................................. 71
Maryland .......................................... 290
Massachusetts ..................................... 764
Michigan .......................................... 616
Minnesota ......................................... 346
Mississippi ....................................... 61
Missouri .......................................... 340
Montana ........................................... 72
Nebraska .......................................... 80
Nevada ............................................ 115
New Hampshire ..................................... 97
New Jersey ........................................ 1,101
New Mexico ........................................ 93
New York .......................................... 2,662
North Carolina .................................... 193
North Dakota ...................................... 42
Ohio .............................................. 659
Oklahoma .......................................... 196
Oregon ............................................ 271
Pennsylvania ...................................... 927
Rhode Island ...................................... 107
South Carolina .................................... 96
South Dakota ...................................... 35
Tennessee ......................................... 183
Texas ............................................. 1,317
Utah .............................................. 124
Vermont ........................................... 42
Virginia .......................................... 327
Washington ........................................ 491
West Virginia ..................................... 36
Wisconsin ......................................... 361
Wyoming ........................................... 43
Total ............................................. 22,433
```

I.A.T.A. COUNT OF
CANADIAN TRAVEL AGENCIES
(as of September 30, 1983)

Alberta	328
British Columbia	482
Manitoba	116
New Brunswick	29
Newfoundland	18
Northwest Territory	5
Nova Scotia	48
Ontario	1,364
Prince Edward Island	7
Quebec	511
Saskatchewan	72
Yukon	4
Total	2,982

EXPANDING YOUR TRAVEL EDUCATION

How often have you heard it said that "half the fun was getting there?" In no place does this old adage hold more truth than in the field of travel. Think back to your childhood when your family planned a trip away from home. Wasn't the anticipation of new adventure the source of great excitement? Didn't you try to imagine what your destination would be like? And wasn't the family "a-buzz" with talk of where to stay, what to see, and what to wear?

You will receive the same thrill of anticipation from your education in travel. Someone recently asked, "Ben, how much will I have to know before I become an expert?" I could only reply with the old Chinese riddle, "How long is a string?" My point was that the *learning* about travel should become an adventure all its own.

Unlike most jobs, which can become monotonous soon after they are learned, travel is as varied and unpredictable as the people who inhabit our planet. In order to help you broaden your knowledge of travel, I have listed many resources available to you. While every attempt has been made to be as accurate as possible, it is advisable that you write or call those sources that are of interest to you before sending any money. In regard to the schools listed, state education bureaus and accrediting agencies should also be consulted. Should you find a school that moved, closed down, or modified its curriculum, please write to Prima Publishing and Communications. All corrections, additions, and deletions will be included in future editions.

TRAVEL TRADE PUBLICATIONS IN THE UNITED STATES AND CANADA

Agent West Traveler (Canada)
Bizletter Publishing, Ltd.
1256 W. Pender
Vancouver, British Columbia, Canada

A.S.T.A. Travel News
488 Madison Ave.
New York, New York 10022

Business Travel
Travel Trade Publications, Inc.
6 E. 46th St.
New York, New York 10017

CTM Weekly Bulletin (Canada)
Concepts Travel Media, Ltd.
Box 575, Sta. F
Toronto, Ontario, Canada M4Y 2L8

California Travel Report
Freed-Crown Publishing Co.
Box 2047, 6931 Van Nuys Blvd.
Van Nuys, California 91405

Canadian Travel Courier (Canada)
Maclean-Hunter, Ltd.
481 University Ave.
Toronto, Ontario, Canada M5W 1A7

Canadian Travel News (Canada)
Southam Business Publications, Inc.
1450 Don Mills Rd.
Don Mills, Ontario, Canada M3B 2X7

Canadian Travel Press (Canada)
Baxter Publishing
100 Adelaide W., Suite 1300
Toronto, Ontario, Canada M5H 1S3

Cruises & Tours Everywhere
Cruises & Tours, Inc.
250 W. 57th St.
New York, New York 10019

Hotel & Travel Index
Ziff-Davis Publishing Co.
One Park Ave.
New York, New York 10016

Incentive Travel Ideas
International Travel Assoc.
1601 22nd St., Suite 404
West Des Moines, Iowa 50265

Incentive Travel International
Harcourt Brace Jovanovich
  Publications
757 3rd Ave.
New York, New York 10017

Incentive Travel Manager
Brentwood Publishing Corp.
825 S. Barrington Ave.
Los Angeles, California 90049

Institute of Certified
  Travel Agents Newsletter
I.C.T.A. P.O. Box 56
Wellesley, Massachusetts 02181

International Association of
  Tour Managers Newsletter
100 Bank St., Suite 3J
New York, New York 10014

Jax Fax Travel Marketing
Jet Airtransport Exchange, Inc.
280 Tokeneke Rd.
Darien, Connecticut 06820

Journal of Travel Research
Business Research Division
Campus Box 420
University of Colorado
Boulder, Colorado 80309

Le Traveller & Travel Industry
  Reporter (Canada)
Fundy Group Publications, Ltd.
Box 128
Yarmouth, Nova Scotia,
Canada B5A 4B2

Marketing Voyages (Canada)
Les Publications Verd, Ltee.
6841 St. Hubert
Montreal, Quebec, Canada H2S 2M8

Meeting News
Gralla Publications
1515 Broadway
New York, New York 10036

Meetings and Conventions
Ziff-Davis Publishing Co., Inc.
One Park Ave.
New York, New York 10016

OAG Pocket Flight Guide
Official Airline Guide, Inc.
2000 Clearwater Dr.
Oak Brook, Illinois 60521

OAG Pocket Travel Planner
Official Airline Guide, Inc.
2000 Clearwater Dr.
Oak Brook, Illinois 60521

OAG Travel Planner &
  Hotel & Motel Guide
Official Airline Guide, Inc.
2000 Clearwater Dr.
Oak Brook, Illinois 60521

OAG Travel Planner & Hotel &
  Motel Guide, European Edition
Official Airline Guide, Inc.
2000 Clearwater Dr.
Oak Brook, Illinois 60521

OAG Worldwide Cruise &
  Shipline Guide
Official Airline Guide, Inc.
2000 Clearwater Dr.
Oak Brook, Illinois 60521

OAG Worldwide Tour Guide
Official Airline Guide, Inc.
2000 Clearwater Dr.
Oak Brook, Illinois 60521

Official Airline Guide,
  North American Edition
Official Airline Guide, Inc.
2000 Clearwater Dr.
Oak Brook, Illinois 60521

Official Airline Guide,
  Worldwide Edition
Official Airline Guide, Inc.
2000 Clearwater Dr.
Oak Brook, Illinois 60521

Official Steamship Guide
International Transportation
  Guides, Inc.
111 Cherry St.
New Canaan, Connecticut 06840

Pacific Hotel Directory &
  Travel Guide
Pacific Area Travel Association
228 Grant Ave.
San Francisco, California 94108

Pacific Travel News
Western Business Publications
  for the Pacific Area Travel
  Association
274 Brannan St.
San Francisco, California 94107

Personal Service Guide
Travel Trade Publications
6 E. 46th St.
New York, New York 10017

Travel Agent
American Traveler, Inc.
2 W. 46th St.
New York, New York 10036

Travel Agents Marketplace
  (Travel Agents Guide)
Gralla Publications
1515 Broadway
New York, New York 10036

Travel Digest
Transatlantic Publishing Corp.
342 Madison Ave.
New York, New York 10017

Travel Marketing and Agency
  Management Guidelines
Armin D. Lehmann Associates, Inc.
309 Santa Monica Blvd., Suite 304
Santa Monica, California 90401

Travel Routes Around the World
  (Freighter)
Harian Publishing
1 Vernon Ave.
Floral Park, New York 11740

Travel Trade Magazine
Travel Trade Publications, Inc.
6 E. 46th St.
New York, New York 10017

Travel Trade Newspaper
Travel Trade Publications, Inc.
6 E. 46th St.
New York, New York 10017

Travel Weekly
Ziff-Davis Publishing Co.
One Park Ave.
New York, New York 10016

TravelAge East and
  TravelAge Southeast
888 7th Ave.
New York, New York 10106

TravelAge MidAmerica
2416 Prudential Plaza
Chicago, Illinois 60601

TravelAge West
582 Market St., Room 603
San Francisco, California 94104

Travelscene
888 7th Ave.
New York, New York 10019

Travelweek Bulletin (Canada)
Concepts Travel Media, Ltd.
P.O. Box 575, Station F
Toronto, Ontario, Canada M4Y 2L8

Worldwide Meetings & Incentives
757 3rd Ave.
New York, New York 10017

SCHOOLS:
TRAVEL AND TRADE SCHOOLS, COLLEGES, AND UNIVERSITIES WHICH OFFER TRAVEL-AGENCY-RELATED PROGRAMS

ALASKA

Alaska Business College
5159 Old Seward Hwy.
Anchorage 99503
Tel.: (907) 277-2601

Cardinal School of Travel
2437 Ingra
Anchorage 99504
Tel.: (907) 277-6090

Sheldon Jackson College
P.O. Box 479
Sitka 99835
Tel: (907) 747-5221

ARIZONA

Chaparral Career College
5001 E. Speedway
Tucson 85712
Tel.: (602) 327-6866

Maricopa Technical Community
  College
106 E. Washington St.
Phoenix 85003
Tel.: (602) 258-7251

Phoenix College
1202 W. Thomas Rd.
Phoenix 85013
Tel.: (602) 264-2492

Pima Community College
50 Speedway Blvd.
Tucson 85705
Tel.: (602) 884-6666

SST Travel Schools
2538 E. University Dr.
Phoenix 85034

SST Travel Schools
7975 N. Hayden Rd., Suite B-121
Scottsdale 85258
Tel: (602) 998-0776

Western International University
10202 N. 19th Ave.
Phoenix 85021
Tel.: (602) 943-2311

ARKANSAS

South Central Career College
3901 McCain Park Dr.
North Little Rock 72116
Tel.: (501) 758-6800

CALIFORNIA

Academy International
1520 State St.
Santa Barbara 93101

Academy Pacific
191 S. E St.
San Bernardino 92401

American Business College -
  Technical Division
5952 El Cajon Blvd.
San Diego 92115

California State Polytechnic
  University
3801 W. Temple
Pomona 91768
Tel.: (714) 598-4592

Canada College
Retail Travel Agent Program
4200 Farm Hill Blvd.
Redwood City 94061
Tel.: (415) 364-1212

Chabot College
South Community College District
25555 Hesperian Blvd.
Hayward 94545
Tel.: (415) 895-9807

Coastline Community College
10231 Slater Ave.
Fountain Valley 92708
Tel.: (714) 963-0824

Columbia College
P.O. Box 1849
Columbia 95310

Condie College
1 W. Campbell
Campbell 95008-1096
Tel.: (408) 866-6666

Echols International Travel
  Training Courses, Inc.
12401 Wilshire Blvd., Suite 305
Los Angeles, 90025

Echols International Travel
  Training Course, Inc.
1390 Market St., Suite 218
San Francisco 94102
Tel.: (415) 861-1922

Foothill College
12345 El Monte Rd.
Los Altos Hills 94022
Tel.: (415) 948-8590

Fullerton College
321 E. Chapman Ave.
Fullerton 92634
Tel.: (714) 871-8000

Great World Travel College
760 Market St., Suite 546
San Francisco 94102
Tel.: (415) 391-1726

International Airline & Travel
  Career & Personnel School
P.O. Box 2129 Airport Station
Oakland 94614
Tel.: (415) 632-7355

International Career Academy
5612 Van Nuys Blvd.
Van Nuys 91401

International College of Travel
166 Grant Ave., 6th Fl.
San Francisco 94108
Tel.: (415) 398-0771

Los Angeles Airport College Center
9700 S. Sepulveda Blvd.
Los Angeles 90045
Tel.: (213) 776-5264

Los Angeles City College
855 N. Vermont Ave.
Los Angeles 90029
Tel.: (213) 663-9141

Mount San Antonio College
1100 N. Grand Ave.
Walnut 91789
Tel.: (714) 594-5611

North American Correspondence
  Schools
4401 Birch St.
Newport Beach 92660

Orange Coast Jr. College
2701 Fairview Rd.
Costa Mesa 92626
Tel.: (714) 556-5651

Pacific Travel School
610 E. 17th St.
Santa Ana 92701
Tel.: (714) 543-9495

Palomar Community College
1140 W. Mission Rd.
San Marcos 92069
Tel.: (714) 744-1150

Pasadena City College
Travel Service Operations
1570 E. Colorado Blvd.
Pasadena 91106
Tel.: (213) 578-7073

Platt College
6250 El Cajon Blvd.
San Diego 92115
Tel.: (714) 265-0107

Saddleback College
28000 Marguerite Pkwy.
Mission Viejo 92692
Tel.: (714) 831-4500

San Diego City College
1313 Twelfth St.
San Diego 92101
Tel.: (714) 238-1181

San Diego Mesa College
7250 Mesa College Dr.
San Diego 92111
Tel.: (714) 279-2300

San Diego Miramar College
10440 Black Mountain Rd.
San Diego 92126
Tel.: (714) 271-7300

154

San Francisco School of Travel
660 Sacramento St., Suite 300
San Francisco 94111
Tel.: (415) 956-5622

Santa Ana College
17th at Bristol
Santa Ana 92706
Tel.: (714) 835-3000

School of Travel
12504 Riverside Dr.
North Hollywood 91607

Simi Valley Adult School
3150 School St.
Simi Valley 93065

Southwestern Community College
900 Otay Lakes Rd.
Chula Vista 92010
Tel.: (714) 421-6700

SST Travel Schools, Inc.
7801 Mission Center Ct., Suite 100
San Diego 92108
Tel.: (714) 298-0890

Travel Advisors Training Academy,
   Ltd.
3960 Wilshire Blvd., No. 205
Los Angeles 90010

Travel Concepts International
937 Howe Ave.
Sacramento 95825
Tel.: (916) 920-4047

Travel Concepts International
1700 N. Broadway, Suite 206
Walnut Creek 94596

Travel Dimensions Travel Training
6363 Auburn Blvd., Suite C
Citrus Heights 95610
Tel.: (916) 969-8666

Travel Experts Training School
Mercado Del Sol Shopping Center
731 S. Hwy. 101
Solano Beach 92075

Travel University International
1936 Quivira Way
San Diego 92109
Tel.: (619) 222-3915

Tri-Cities Regional
   Occupational Program
9401 S. Painter Ave.
Whittier 90605

University of California Extension
Travel Agent Training Program
Santa Cruz 95060

U.S. International University
10455 Pomerado Rd.
San Diego 92131
Tel.: (714) 271-4300

Vista College
2020 Milvia St.
Berkeley 94704
Tel.: (415) 841-8431

West Los Angeles City College
Airport College Center
The Travel Programme
9700 S. Sepulveda Blvd.
Los Angeles 90045

COLORADO

Colorado School of Travel
850 Kipling St.
Lakewood 80215
Tel.: (303) 233-8654

Mountain States Travel
   Training Institute, Inc.
14001 E. Iliff Ave.
Aurora 80014
Tel.: (303) 695-1947

Parks College, Inc.
7350 Broadway
Denver 80221
Tel.: (303) 426-1808

Pathways Travel Service, Inc.
2625 28th St.
Boulder 80301
Tel.: (303) 449-0099

SST Travel Schools, Inc.
14291 E. Fourth Ave., Bldg. 7
Aurora 80011
Tel.: (303) 363-8103

Travel Trade School of Boulder
1966 13th St., Suite B
Boulder 80303
Tel.: (303) 442-6466

Travel Trade School of
   Colorado Springs
2812 E. Bijou St., Suite 102
Colorado Springs 80909
Tel.: (303) 630-1717

Travel Trade School, Inc.
609 W. Littleton Blvd., Suite 201
Littleton 80120
Tel.: (303) 795-1825

Travel Training School
7710 Ralston Rd.
Arvada 80002

Travel Training School
8333 Greenwood
Denver 80221
Tel.: (303) 452-9666

CONNECTICUT

Branford Hall School of Business
19 S. Main St.
Branford 06405
Tel.: (203) 488-2525

Briarwood School for Women
2279 Mt. Vernon Rd.
Southington 06489
Tel.: (203) 628-4751

Connecticut Academy
11-13 W. Washington St.
(P.O. Box 817)
Norwalk 06854
Tel.: (203) 838-0286

Connecticut School of Electronics
586 Boulevard (P.O. Box 7308)
New Haven 06519
Tel.: (203) 624-2121

County Schools, Inc.
3787 Main St. (P.O. Box 6278)
Bridgeport 06606
Tel.: (203) 374-6187

Fugazy International Travel School
100 Melrose Square
Greenwich 06830

Fugazy International Travel School
Kingsley St. & Columbus Blvd.
Hartford 06103
Tel.: (203) 728-6680

Fugazy International Travel School
67 Whitney Ave.
New Haven 06510
Tel.: (203) 772-0470

Fugazy International Travel School
15 Huntington Plaza
Shelton 06484

Fugazy International Travel School
581 Chase Ave.
Waterbury 06710

Huntington Institute
204 State St.
North Haven 06473
Tel.: (203) 288-8945

Huntington Institute
193 Broadway
Norwich 06360
Tel.: (203) 886-0507

University of Hartford,
   Div. of Continuing Education
200 Bloomfield Ave.
Hartford 06117

University of New Haven
Admissions Office
West Haven 06516

Van Dyke Travel Academy
60 Temple St.
New Haven 06510

DELAWARE

New Castle County
   Vocational-Technical
   School District
1417 Newport Rd.
Wilmington 19804
Tel.: (302) 995-8000

DISTRICT OF COLUMBIA

International Travel
   Training Courses, Inc.
5100 Wisconsin Ave. N.W., Suite 200
Washington, D.C. 20016
Tel.: (202) 363-1288

World Travel Training Courses
4818 MacArthur Blvd. N.W.
Washington, D.C. 20007
Tel.: (202) 965-7200

FLORIDA

All Seasons Travel Services, Inc.
299 W. Granada Blvd.
Ormond Beach 32074
Tel.: (904) 677-7722

All Seasons Travel Services, Inc.
412 Club House Dr., Suite D
Palm Coast 32037
Tel.: (904) 445-5633

Associated Schools, Inc.
1110 N.E. 163rd St.
Miami 33162

Florida International University
Tamiami Campus
Miami 33199

Florida Travel Careers School
2413 N. Wickman Rd.
Melbourne 32935
Tel.: (305) 725-9097

Gruber Travel Training Institute, Inc.
2809 Bird Ave.
Miami 33133
Tel.: (305) 445-8530

Miami Springs Adult Center
751 Dove Ave.
Miami Springs 33166

Mirror Lake/Tomlinson
  Adult Education Center
709 Mirror Lake Dr. N.
St. Petersburg 33701

New Image Center
3918 E. Hillsborough Ave., Suite 100
Tampa 33610
Tel.: (813) 238-6441

Prospect Hall College
1725 Monroe St.
Hollywood 33020
Tel.: (305) 923-8100

Seminole Community College
Sanford 32771
Tel.: (305) 323-1450

Seven Seas Travel Sales School
3801 N. University Dr.
Sunrise 33321
Tel.: (305) 741-7730

Southeastern Academy
2333 E. Spacecoast Pkwy.,
  (P.O. Drawer 1768)
Kissimmee 32741
Tel.: (305) 847-4444

Universal Travel Institute
1950 Courtney Dr.
Fort Myers 33901
Tel: (813) 939-7900

Webber College
Director of Admissions
Babson Park 33827

GEORGIA

Advanced Career Training
2581 Piedmont Rd. N.E.
Suite L020
Atlanta 30324
Tel.: (404) 237-2274

National Business Institute
1776 Peachtree St.
Atlanta 30309
Tel.: (404) 874-3800

Omni School of Travel
6065 Roswell Rd., Suite 712
Atlanta 30328
Tel.: (404) 252-6664

Rutledge College
60 Peachtree Park Dr. N.E.
Atlanta 30309
Tel.: (404) 351-7733

Stevens, Patricia, Business and
  Fashion College
3330 Peachtree Rd. N.E.
Atlanta 30326

HAWAII

Hawaii School of Business
111 N. King St.
Honolulu 96817
Tel.: (808) 524-4014

Travel Institute of the Pacific
1314 S. King St., Suite 1051
Honolulu 96814
Tel.: (808) 531-2708

Traveler's Choice School of Travel
1831 S. King St., Suite 202
Honolulu 96826
Tel.: (808) 946-2191

ILLINOIS

Careers in Travel
239 S. Main St., P.O. Box 1483
Decatur 62525
Tel.: (217) 428-0445

Carroll Travel School
480 Central Ave.
Northfield 60093
Tel.: (312) 446-6161

Daley, Richard J., College
City Colleges of Chicago
7500 S. Pulaski Rd.
Chicago 60652

MacCormac College, Downtown
  Center
327 S. LaSalle St.
Chicago 60604
Tel.: (312) 922-1884

MacCormac College,
  West Suburban Center
5825 St. Charles Rd.
Berkeley 60163
Tel.: (312) 547-5100

Parks College of Aeronautical
  Technology
Cahokia 62206

Regal School of Travel
12232 S. Harlem Ave.
Palos Heights 60463
Tel.: (312) 448-7700

Roberta Fisher Travel School, Inc.
133 W. Wing St.
Arlington Heights 60005

Travel Agency Career Training
301 157th St.
Calumet City 60409

Travel School
625 N. Michigan Ave.
Chicago 60611
Tel.: (312) 664-5655

V.I.P. Travel Agents School
600 N. McClurg Ct., Suite 304A
Chicago 60611
Tel.: (312) 266-1484

Western Illinois University
College of Health, Physical Education,
  and Recreation
Macomb 61455

Winnetka Travel School, Inc.
561 Lincoln Ave.
Winnetka 60093

IOWA

Spencer School of Business
217 W. 5th St.
Spencer 51301
Tel.: (712) 262-7290

KANSAS

Brown-Mackie College
P.O. Box 1587, 126 S. Santa Fe
Salina 67401

Bryan Travel College
1527 Fairlawn Rd.
Topeka 66604
Tel.: (913) 272-7511

Clark College
3600 Topeka Ave.
Topeka 66611

Platt College
5200 W. 110th St.
Overland Park 66211
Tel.: (913) 341-1733

LOUISIANA

Audubon Commercial College
3901 Tulane Ave.
New Orleans 70119
Tel.: (504) 581-3737

Harvey School of Travel
4241 Veterans Blvd.
Metairie 70002
Tel.: (504) 454-2265

Peggy Fineran School of
  Travel Instruction
2107 Causeway Blvd., Suite A
Mandeville 70448
Tel.: (504) 892-7349

158

Sawyer School
2740 Canal St.
New Orleans 70119
Tel.: (504) 821-5881

MARYLAND

Essex Community College
Baltimore County 21237

Executive International Travel School
114 Chartley Blvd.
Reisterstown 21136

Fleet Business School
1939 Lincoln Dr.
Annapolis 21401
Tel.: (301) 268-7511

Harford Community College
401 Thomas Rune Rd.
Bel Air 21014

Triple T Travel School
4915 Aspen Hill Rd.
Rockville 20853
Tel.: (301) 949-9820

MASSACHUSETTS

Becker Junior College
61 Sever St.
Worcester 01609

Central Travel School
P.O. Box 1649, 220 Worthington St.
Springfield 01101
Tel.: (413) 781-1680

Endicott College
Beverly 01915

Institute of Certified Travel Agents
P.O. Box 56
Wellesley 02181
Tel.: (617) 237-0280

Northeast Travel School
227 W. Central St.
Sudbury 01760
Tel.: (617) 655-6800

Robin Hood School of Travel
112 Central
Lynn 01901

Salem Junior College
Salem 01970

Travel Education Center
Harvard Square
93 Mount Auburn St.
Cambridge 02138
Tel.: (617) 547-7750

Travel School and Hotel
   School of America
1047 Commonwealth Ave.
Boston 02215
Tel.: (617) 787-1214

MICHIGAN

American Travel Schools, Inc.
22932 Woodward
Detroit 48220
Tel.: (313) 399-5522

Argubright Business College
37 Capitol Ave. N.E.
Battle Creek 49014
Tel.: (616) 968-6105

Davenport College
415 E. Fulton St.
Grand Rapids 49503
Tel.: (616) 451-3511

Davenport College
4123 W. Main St.
Kalamazoo 49007
Tel.: (616) 382-2835

Davenport College
220 E. Kalamazoo
Lansing 48933
Tel.: (517) 489-5767

Ferris State College
School of Business
   Hospitality Management
Big Rapids 49307

Jewett Career School
920 Long Blvd., Suite 10
Lansing 48910

Port Huron School of Business
511 Fort St., Suite 430
Port Huron 48060
Tel.: (313) 984-5185

MINNESOTA

Dakota County Area Vocational
    Techincal Institute
1300 145th St. E.
Rosemount 55068
Tel.: (612) 423-2281

McConnell School, Inc.
831 Second Ave. S.
Minneapolis 55402
Tel.: (612) 332-4238

Northern Technical School
    of Business, Inc.
2201 Blaisdell Ave. S.
Minneapolis 55404
Tel.: (612) 874-6414

Rasmussen Business College
15 W. Fifth St.
St. Paul 55102
Tel.: (612) 222-4474

MISSOURI

Park College
Kansas City 64152

Platt College
Ninth and Felix Streets
St. Joseph 64501
Tel.: (816) 233-9563

NEBRASKA

Grand Island School of Business, Inc.
410 W. 2nd St., P.O. Box 399
Grand Island 68801
Tel.: (308) 382-8044

Travel Careers Institute
9777 M. St.
Omaha 68127
Tel.: (402) 339-1200

NEVADA

Reno Business College
258 Wonder St.
Reno 89502
Tel.: (702) 323-4145

NEW JERSEY

Bergen Community College
400 Paramus Rd.
Paramus 07652
Tel.: (201) 447-1500

Career Institute
Avenue A. and 28th Streets
Bayonne 07002

Career Institute
346 Cambridge Rd.
Brick 08723

Career Institute
600 Harristown Rd.
Glen Rock 07452

Career Institute
Memorial Park Dr.
Livingston 07039

Career Institute
Corey Rd.
Mount Olive

Career Institute
266 E. Main St.
Ramsey 07446

Career Institute
125 Kent Place Blvd.
Summit 07901

Empire Technical Schools, Inc.
Central Ave.
East Orange 07018
Tel.: (201) 675-0565

Liberty Travel School
11 Park Place
Paramus 07652
Tel.: (201) 967-3123

O'Brien's Travel School
Allendale Shopping Center
Allendale 07401
Tel.: (201) 825-3530

Professional School of Business
Bergen Mall, U.S. Rt. 4
Paramus 07652

Professional School of Business
2583 Morris Ave.
Union 07083
Tel.: (201) 687-8633

Professional School of Business
1479 U.S. Rt. 23
Wayne 07470

Sutton School
900 Haddon Ave.
Collingswood 08107
Tel.: (609) 858-7009

Taylor Business Institute
Routes 22 & 28, Box 6875
Bridgewater 08807
Tel.: (201) 231-1249

Taylor Business Institute
2444 Rt. 34
Manasquan 08736
Tel.: (201) 528-7363

Taylor Business Institute
1003B Greentree, Executive
   Campus, Rt. 73
Marlton 08053
Tel.: (609) 983-8307

Taylor Business Institute
Rt. 17 and Buehler Place
Paramus 07652
Tel.: (201) 967-8880

Taylor Business Institute
White Horse Pike, P.O. Box 815
Pomona 08240
Tel.: (609) 652-0444

Taylor International Business
   Institute
41 Newark St.
Hoboken 07030
Tel.: (201) 656-6185

The Travel School
Center Point Plaza,
   Tilton Rd. and Rt. 9
Northfield 08225
Tel.: (609) 767-0011

The Travel School
212 L'Villa Shopping and
   Professional Center, Rt. 73
West Berlin 08091
Tel.: (609) 767-0011

Travel Institute, Inc.
910 Bergen Ave.
Jersey City 07306
Tel.: (201) 420-7855

Union County Technical Institute
   and Vocational Center
1776 Raritan Rd.
Scotch Plains 07076
Tel.: (201) 889-2000

Woodbridge Travel School
831 Rahway Ave.
Woodbridge 07095

NEW YORK CITY

American Society of Travel Agents
711 5th Ave.
New York 10022
Tel.: (212) 486-0700

Eastern School
154 W. 14th St.
New York 10011
Tel.: (212) 675-6655

Empress School of Travel
293 Madison Ave.
New York 10017
Tel.: (212) 697-8698

Fugazy International School of
   Travel
645 Madison Ave.
New York 10022
Tel.: (212) 759-1012

Latin American School, Inc.
130 W. 42nd St., 10th Floor
New York 10036
Tel.: (212) 391-0032

Long Island University
Brooklyn Center, University Plaza
Brooklyn 11201
Tel.: (212) 834-6000

New School for Social Research
66 5th Ave.
New York 10011

Pan American School of Travel
159 W. 33rd St.
New York 10001
Tel.: (212) 947-9800

Pohs Institute
150 Nassau St.
New York 10038
Tel.: (212) 267-7318

Sobelsohn School
1540 Broadway
New York 10036
Tel.: (212) 575-1500

Taylor Business Institute
55 W. 42nd St.
New York 10117
Tel.: (212) 279-0510

Travel Institute, Inc.
15 Park Row
New York 10038
Tel.: (212) 349-3331

NEW YORK STATE

Adelphi University
Garden City 11530

Bryant and Stratton Business
  Institute
1028 Main St.
Buffalo 14202
Tel.: (716) 884-9120

Bryant and Stratton Business
  Institute
200 Bryant and Stratton Way
Williamsville 14221
Tel.: (716) 631-0260

Genesee Community College
1 College Rd.
Batavia 14020
Tel.: (716) 343-0055

Herkimer County Community
  College
Reservoir Rd.
Herkimer 14020

Jefferson Community College
P.O. Box 473
Watertown 13601

McGregor School for Travel Agents
190 E. Post Rd.
White Plains 10601
Tel.: (914) 761-1279

Niagara University
Niagara Falls 14109

Pequa Travel School
915 N. Broadway
Massapequa 11758

Pohs Institute
362-B Mid-Island Shopping Plaza
Hicksville 11802
Tel.: (516) 381-5050

Pohs Institute
Coachman Hotel
123 E. Post Rd.
White Plains 10601

Sawyer School
845 Central Ave.
Albany 12206
Tel.: (518) 438-2022

Skinner, Alice B., School
200 Garden City Plaza
Garden City 11530
Tel.: (516) 747-4443

Taylor Business Institute
196 Fulton Ave., P.O. Box 367
Hempstead 11551
Tel.: (516) 483-8855

Tompkins-Courtland Community
  College
170 North St.
Dryden 13053

Weymouth Business Institute
196 Fulton Ave.
Hempstead 11550
Tel.: (516) 483-8855

NORTH CAROLINA

Asheboro College
151 N. Fayetteville St.
Asheboro 27203
Tel.: (919) 625-4560

Cecils Junior College
1567 Patton Ave.
Asheville 28806
Tel.: (704) 252-2486

Rutledge College
P.O. Box 32803
Charlotte 28232
Tel.: (704) 332-2625

OHIO

American Travel Agents School
29001 Cedar Rd.
Lyndhurst 44124

American Travel Agents School
c/o Holiday Inn, Room 106
1100 Crocker Rd.
Westlake 44145
Tel.: (216) 835-0888

Columbus Paraprofessional
  Institute
70 Robinwood Ave.
Columbus 43213
Tel.: (614) 221-4481

Columbus Paraprofessional
  Institute
1516 W. Broad St.
Columbus 43222
Tel.: (614) 279-3319

Sawyer College of Business
13027 Lorain Ave.
Cleveland 44111
Tel.: (216) 941-7666

Sawyer College of Business
3150 Mayfield Rd.
Cleveland Heights 44118
Tel.: (216) 932-0911

Travel Agents Training School
5356 Pearl Rd.
Cleveland 44129
Tel.: (216) 845-0304; 845-2627

Traveline School of Travel
18615 Detroit Ave.
Lakewood 44107
Tel.: (216) 226-0380

United Career School
1098 E. Bible Rd.
Lima 45802

OKLAHOMA

DeArmond-Young School of Travel
2913 N.W. 122nd St.
Oklahoma City 73120
Tel.: (405) 755-6460

International Travel Institute
5001 E. 68th St., Suite 530
Tulsa 74136
Tel.: (918) 429-4427

Oklahoma School of Business
  and Technology
4770 S. Harvard Ave.
Tulsa 74135

OREGON

Northwest Schools
1221 N.W. 21st St.
Portland 97209
Tel.: (503) 226-4811

Northwestern College of Business
1950 S.W. 6th Ave.
Portland 97201
Tel.: (503) 224-6410

SST Travel Schools
6627 N.E. 82nd Ave.
Portland 97220
Tel.: (503) 255-5627

Western Business College
505 S.W. 6th Ave.
Portland 97204
Tel.: (503) 222-3225

PENNSYLVANIA

Aero Travel Career Training
1010 Jefferson St.
Latrobe 15650
Tel.: (412) 537-9348

Allentown Business School
Center Square Building
11 N. 7th St.
Allentown 18101
Tel.: (215) 432-4371

Allied Business Institute
1920 Chestnut St.
Philadelphia 19103
Tel.: (215) 561-5800

Boyd, Wilma, Career Schools, Inc.
On the Plaza, Chatham Center
Pittsburgh 15219
Tel.: (412) 456-1800

Business Skills Center
1516 Spruce St.
Philadelphia 19102
Tel.: (215) 545-2800

Central Pennsylvania Business
  School
College Hill
Summerdale 17903

Harcum Junior College
Bryn Mawr 19010

163

International School of Travel, Inc.
21 S. 12th St.
Philadelphia 19107
Tel.: (215) 568-0560

Martin School of Business
2417 Welsh Rd.
Philadelphia 19114
Tel.: (215) 677-6110

New Castle Business College
316 Rhodes Place
New Castle 16101

Palmer School
1118 Market St.
Philadelphia 19107
Tel.: (215) 568-3800

Rittenhouse Academy
1516 Spruce St.
Philadelphia 19102
Tel.: (215) 545-2800

Talmage Travel School
1223 Walnut St.
Philadelphia 19107

Travel School, Inc.
1525 Walnut St.
Philadelphia 19102
Tel.: (215) 568-7676

RHODE ISLAND

Bryant College of Business
   Administration
Smithfield 02917

Johnson and Wales College
8 Abbott Park Place
Providence 02903
Tel.: (401) 456-1000

Sawyer School
101 Main St.
Pawtucket 02860
Tel.: (401) 272-8400

Travel School of America
Jordan Marsh Co.
Warwick Mall
Warwick 02888
Tel.: (401) 738-0100

SOUTH DAKOTA

Dakota State College
Madison 57042

National College of Business
P.O. Box 1780, 321 Kansas City St.
Rapid City 57709
Tel.: (605) 394-4800

TENNESSEE

American Traveler Travel Agent
   School
111 Racine St.
Memphis 38111

TEXAS

Braniff Education Systems, Inc.
3113 S. University Dr.,
   P.O. Box 11552
Fort Worth 76109
Tel.: (817) 926-7851

Capitol City Trade and Technical
   School
205 E. Riverside Dr.
Austin 78704
Tel.: (512) 444-3257

Capitol City Trade and Technical
   School
5424 Highway 290 W.
Austin 78735
Tel.: (512) 444-3257

International Aviation
   and Travel Academy
1201 N. Watson Rd., Suite 270,
   P.O. Box 5272
Arlington 76011
Tel.: (817) 640-0553

International Aviation
   and Travel Academy
7326 Aviation Place
Dallas 75235
Tel.: (214) 358-7295

International Travel Institute
6300 Hillcroft, Suite 114
Houston 77081
Tel.: (713) 777-0147

International Travel Institute
224 N. Story, Suite 138
Irving 75061

UTAH

Brigham Young University
Provo 84602

Bryman Schools, Inc.
445 S. 300 E.
Salt Lake City 84111
Tel.: (801) 521-2830

VIRGINIA

American Transportation Institute, Inc.
8224 Old Courthouse Rd.
Vienna 22180

C.I. Travel School
250 Janat Plaza
Norfolk 23502
Tel.: (804) 461-6800

Commonwealth College
710 W. Mercury Blvd.
Hampton 23666
Tel.: (804) 838-2122

European-American Travel Training, Inc.
7639 Leesburg Pike
Falls Church 22043

Kottner Travel Institute
2600 Buford Rd.
Richmond 23235

Northern Virginia Community College
3001 N. Beauregard St.
Alexandria 22311
Tel.: (703) 323-3000

Northern Virginia Community College
8333 Little River Turnpike, Rt. 236
Annandale 22003
Tel.: (703) 323-3000

Northern Virginia Community College, Loudoun Campus
1000 Harry Flood Byrd Hwy.
Sterling 22170
Tel.: (703) 323-3000

Red Carpet Travel Service
2600 Buford Rd.
Richmond 23235

Simmons, Cal, Travel School, Dalton Wharf
107 Oronoco St.
Alexandria 22314
Tel.: (703) 549-8650

WASHINGTON

Chase Business College
2700 N.E. Andersen Rd., Suites D2-D5
Vancouver 98661
Tel.: (206) 693-4717

Clover Park Vocational Technical Institute
4500 Steilacoom Blvd. S.W.
Tacoma 98499
Tel.: (206) 584-7611

Edmonds Community College
2000 68th Ave.
Lynwood 98036

Fox Travel Institute
18000 Pacific Hwy. S. #411
Seattle 98188
Tel.: (206) 433-8550

Highline Community College
240 and Pacific Hwy.
South Midway 98031
Tel.: (206) 878-3710

International Air Academy, Inc.
400 E. Evergreen Blvd.
Vancouver 98660
Tel.: (206) 695-2500

Knapp College of Business
8 Auburn Way N.
Auburn 98002
Tel.: (206) 833-4560

Knapp College of Business
1001 J. St. N.
Tacoma 98403
Tel.: (206) 572-3933

SST Travel Schools, Inc.
15215 52nd Ave. S.
Seattle 98188
Tel.: (206) 244-9200
    (800) 426-5200

165

Travel Central, Inc.
530 Joseph Vance Bldg.
Seattle 98101
Tel.: (206) 682-1142

Travel Institute
1331 3rd Ave.
Seattle 98101
Tel.: (206) 682-6406

Western Business College
6625 E. Mill Plain Blvd.
Vancouver 98661

WISCONSIN

Gateway Technical Institute
Racine Campus
1001 S. Main St.
Racine 53403
Tel.: (414) 631-7300

WYOMING

Matz Career School, Inc.
1744 S. Poplar
Caspar 82601

PUERTO RICO

Instituto de Banca
Avenida Munoz Rivera 996
Rio Piedras 00925
Tel.: (809) 765-8687

Instituto de Comercio e Technologia
703 Avenida Ponce de Leon
Santurce 00907
Tel.: (809) 722-6929

CANADA

University of Manitoba
Winnipeg, Manitoba R3T 2N2

Ryerson Polytechnical Institute
50 Gould St.
Toronto, Ontario M5B 1E8

Sir Sanford Fleming College
Peterborough, Ontario K9J 7B1

166

The
ABCs
of travel

•

**A glossary of the terms
and abbreviations peculiar
to the travel industry**

The growth of an industry, like the growth of a nation, invariably leads to the development of a special language, a set of terms peculiar to that particular industry. And, having developed their own language, the members of that industry proceed, invariably, to vernacularize it—usually with abbreviations.

—Elbi's Law of Industrial Semantics

The ABCs of Travel is a publication of

Travel Weekly

The National Newspaper of the Travel Industry

AAA—(see American Automobile Association)

AAR—(see Association of American Railroads)

ABC—ABC World Airway Guide, an airline tariff published in the U.K.

ABC—Advance Booking Charter. Eliminated by the CAB with the introduction of the Public Charter, but the term continues to be used by some foreign governments and people in the trade.

Absorption—The acceptance by a carrier of a joint fare portion which is less than the amount it would have received for the same service in the absence of such a joint rate.

ABTA—(see Association of British Travel Agents)

ACAP—(see Aviation Consumer Action Project)

ACTA—(see Alliance of Canadian Travel Associations).

Adjoining Rooms—Two or more hotel rooms located side by side but without private connecting doors. Rooms may be adjoining without connecting.

Advertised Tour—Any travel program for which a brochure has been prepared. Specifically, a tour which meets airline requirements for an Inclusive Tour number.

Aeronautical Radio Inc. (ARINC)—A company owned primarily by the airlines that provides communications services for them. Among other things, it provides an electronic switching system which transfers millions of messages from one airline to another each day, and in this way permits each airline to provide confirmed reservations on behalf of all other participating carriers.

Affinity Group—An organization, formed for virtually any purpose other than travel, which subsequently elects to sponsor group travel programs on scheduled or charter aircraft for and at the pro-rata expense of individual members. Clubs, schools, companies, trade associations, religious organizations, etc. are all affinity groups if they fall within certain limits established by the CAB.

Aft—Near, toward or in the stern of a vessel.

AFTA—(see Australian Federation of Travel Agents)

Agency—Apart from its broader meanings: (1) the business place of a retail travel agent; (2) an administrative arm of a government as the Federal Aviation Agency. (see Agent)

Agency Manager—(1) The person who manages a travel or other agency. (2) A carrier or hotel employee who directs sales efforts to wholesalers and travel agents.

Agency Rep—A sales person who calls on travel agents.

Agency Tour—(see Familiarization Tour)

Agent—Broadly, one who acts or has the power to act; more usually, one that acts for or as the representative of another. Most frequently in travel, a specific kind of agent as: (1) a retail travel agent; (2) a carrier employee who sells tickets, a counter or ticket agent; (3) one with broad powers to act for a principal, a general agent; (4) more usually outside the U.S. and Canada: anyone in the travel business other than a principal—a retail travel agent, receiving agent or local operator, a wholesaler.

AGTE—(see Association of Group Travel Executives)

AH&MA—(see American Hotel & Motel Association)

Airline Codes—The system of abbreviations for airlines, airports, fares, etc., used by airlines and travel agents throughout the world. Airline codes are not included in this compendium.

Air Line Pilots Association—(1) Principal labor union of U.S. commercial pilots, co-pilots, flight engineers, etc. U.S. ALPA also has a cabin-service division. (2) Any of 64 national commercial pilots unions, all of which are affiliated in the International Federation of Air Line Pilots Associations.

Airline Rep—A salesman for an airline.

Air-Sea—An adjective describing a cruise or travel program in which one or more transportation legs are provided by air and one or more by sea. Often combined with hotel arrangements.

Air-Taxi—A small aircraft operator of nonscheduled, charter or "on-demand" service.

Air Traffic Conference—A division of the Air Transport Association entrusted with the establishment of standards and working agreements covering the way the domestic airlines deal with each other and the way that the domestic airline industry as a whole deals with international airlines and other segments of the travel industry including travel agents.

Air Transport Association of America—The trade association of U.S. and Canadian (as associate members) scheduled airlines including international, trunk, local service, intra-Hawaiian and Intra-Alaskan, helicopter and cargo carriers.

Air Transport Association of Canada—A trade association of Canadian airlines.

AITO—The Association of Incentive Travel Operators is a national organization of travel firms whose major service is travel incentive programs for business and industry.

A la Carte—According to the bill of fare; with a separate price for each item on the menu. (see Prix Fixe and Table d'Hote)

Alcove—An area, usually for sleeping, set off from a larger room.

All Expense Tour—A tour offering all or most services—transportation, lodging, meals, porterage, sightseeing, etc.—for a pre-established price. The terms "all-expense" and "all-inclusive" are much misused. Virtually no tour rate covers everything. The terms and conditions of a tour contract should specify exactly what is covered.

Alliance of Canadian Travel Associations—A federation of provincial trade associations in Canada.

All-In—British vernacular for all-expense or all-inclusive.

All-Inclusive—(see All Expense Tour)

ALPA—(see Air Line Pilots Association)

AMAV—(see Asociacion Mexicana de Agencias de Viajes)

American Automobile Association—An organization which provides its members with a variety of services—travel information, highway and legal services, insurance, etc.—related to owning and operating automobiles. AAA also operates AAA Worldwide Travel, a multibranch retail and wholesale travel agency organization.

American Bus Association—A trade association representing intercity and charter bus companies.

American Hotel & Motel Association—A federation of state and regional lodging industry trade associations covering the U.S., Canada, Mexico and Central and South America.

American Plan—A hotel rate that includes a bed and three meals. (see Modified American Plan)

American Sightseeing Association—An international trade association of local tour operators. American Sightseeing International (ASI) is a promotional and business name owned by the parent association.

American Society of Travel Agents—The leading trade association of U.S. travel agents and tour operators.

170

Amtrak—The name under which the National Railroad Passenger Corporation operates almost all U.S. intercity passenger trains. The intercity trains are usually operated under contract with individual railroads.

ANTOR—(see Assembly of National Tourist Office Representatives)

AP—(see American Plan)

Apex—Advance purchase excursion. (see Domestic and International Airline Classes of Service)

Apollo—Name of United Airlines' reservation system.

Appointment—Official designation to act as a sales outlet for a carrier, conference or group of hotels. Conferences appoint travel agents; hotel associations and governments appoint wholesalers. (see Fully Appointed)

Arbitrary—An amount published for use only in combination with other air fares for the construction of through fares. Sometimes called a proportional fare.

Area Bank—(see Standard Ticket and Area Bank Settlement Plan)

Areas One, Two and Three—IATA designations for the regions into which it has divided the world for rate- and rule-making purposes. Area One: All of North and South America and the islands adjacent thereto; Greenland, Bermuda, the West Indies and Caribbean Islands, Midway and Palmyra. Area Two: All of Europe (including the USSR west of the Ural Mountains) and the islands adjacent thereto; Iceland, the Azores, all of Africa and the islands adjacent thereto; Ascension Island; the Middle East. Area Three: All of Asia and the islands adjacent thereto except that portion included in Area Two; all of the East Indies, Australia and New Zealand and the islands adjacent thereto; the islands of the Pacific Ocean except those included in Area One. Some of these areas have been subdivided to ease the problem of reaching unanimous agreements among the carriers directly involved. (see TC1, TC2, TC3)

ARTA—(see Association of Retail Travel Agents)

ASI—(see American Sightseeing Association)

Asociacion Mexicana de Agencias de Viajes—Mexican Association of Travel Agencies; an association of Mexican travel agents and tour operators.

Assembly of National Tourist Office Representatives—A professional association of New York City-based executives of foreign government tourist offices.

Association of American Railroads—The trade association of U.S. railroad companies.

Association of British Travel Agents—The principal trade association of travel agents and tour operators in the United Kingdom.

Association of Group Travel Executives—A professional organization of executives responsible for the promotion, sale, operation or purchase of group travel programs.

Association of Retail Travel Agents—A trade association of American travel retailers.

ASTA—(see American Society of Travel Agents)

ATA—(see Air Transport Association)

171

ATAC—(see Air Transport Association of Canada)

ATC—(see Air Traffic Conference)

Australian Federation of Travel Agents—A trade association of travel agents in Australia.

Auto Drop PNR—A passenger name record, stored in a computerized reservation system, that automatically appears in the appropriate queue when it needs to be attended to in some way. For example, if a client is no longer waitlisted, the PNR will appear in the waitlist queue, permitting an agent to inform the client and arrange ticketing. The counselor could then arrange for the PNR to automatically drop into the ticketing queue at a specified future date.

Available (or Availability)—Connotes a conditional status: "Space available", for example, means "if the space is available".

Available Seat Mile—One aircraft seat flown one mile whether occupied or not.

Aviation Consumer Action Project—A Ralph Nader organization that promotes consumer interests before Congress, the courts, the CAB and other governmental agencies dealing with air travel.

Aviation Daily—A Ziff-Davis newsletter published every working day.

Aviation-Space Writers Association—A professional association.

AWA—(see Aviation-Space Writers Association)

B

Back-to-back—Describing a program of multiple air charters between two or more points with arrivals and departures coordinated to eliminate aircraft deadheading and waiting. That is, when one group is delivered at a destination, another is ready to depart from that point.

Back Office Automation—An accounting system for the travel agency that utilizes computers for storage of agency financial data and preparation of business reports. Called back office automation because of its location, it is also often called the agency management system because the programs usually handle more than accounting. They might provide any or all of the following: ticketing, invoice/itinerary preparation, extensive management reports describing client, counselor and supplier dealings with the agency, custom-made statements for clients, and/or word processing and mailing list control.

Baggage Allowance—That weight or volume of baggage that may be carried by a passenger without an additional charge.

Baggage Check—The official receipt issued by a carrier for the luggage of a passenger.

Baggage Tag—Personal identification which must be attached to a piece of luggage checked on an airline.

Balkantourist—The Bulgarian national travel agency.

Bareboat Charter—The rental of a yacht without crew or supplies. (see Provisioned Charter)

Basing Point—A master point, the fares to and from which are established, used in constructing (calculating the amount of) through air fares between other points.

Beam—The breadth of a vessel at its widest part.

Bed-Night—One person spending one night in any hostelry.

Bermuda Plan—Hotel accommodation with full American-style breakfast included in the rate.

Berth—(1) A bed on an airline, ship or railroad car; often, but not necessarily, built in. (2) A space at a wharf for a ship to dock or anchor.

Best Available—(1) A reservation pledging a principal (a) to provide some sort of accommodation and (b) to upgrade the client if possible. (2) A request for a reservation meaning "I'll take anything you have, but I'm willing to pay for your best".

Blocked Space—Reservations, often subject to deposit forfeiture, made with suppliers by wholesalers or travel agents in anticipation of resale.

Bonding—The purchase, for a premium, of a guarantee of protection for a supplier or a customer. In the travel industry, certain bonding programs are mandatory: ATC insists that travel agents be bonded to protect the airlines against defaults; the CAB requires the operators of certain types of charters to carry bonds to protect their customers against default. Some operators and agents buy bonds voluntarily to protect their clients and for promotional purposes.

Bonus—(see Override)

Booking Form—A document which purchasers of tours must complete to give the operator full particulars about who is buying the tour. It states exactly what is being purchased (including options) and must be signed as acknowledgement that the liability clause has been read and understood.

Bow—Fore end of a vessel.

Bow Thruster—A propeller the axis of which is perpendicular to the fore-aft centerline of the ship, which, when employed assists in maneuvering the vessel within close quarters. (see Stabilizer)

Britrail Pass—Railroad pass for visitors to the U.K. offers unlimited Second or First Class transportation (reservations and sleeping facilities extra) for specified numbers of days. Youth passes are available in Second Class only.

Brochure—A printed folder describing a tour or a package and specifying the conditions of the offering.

BTA—British Tourist Authority, the official government travel promotion agency of Great Britain.

Bubble Car—(see Observation Car)

Bulk Fare—Fare available only to tour organizers or operators who purchase a specified block of seats from a carrier at a low, non-commissionable price and then have the responsibility of selling the seats, including a commission in their marked-up price for the seats.

Bulkhead—Any vertical partition, such as the wall of a cabin. There are also watertight and fireproof bulkheads on all modern passenger ships.

Bump—To displace a passenger or guest by virtue of (a) holding a reservation with a higher priority (a regular fare passenger will bump a standby passenger) or (b) being sufficiently important (a Senator can sometimes bump an ordinary passenger, even in first class). A bumped passenger may or may not be entitled to denied boarding compensation depending on the sort of ticket he holds.

Bus—A large highway vehicle for passengers. In the travel industry the word "bus" is reserved for a vehicle that provides scheduled service for an individually-ticketed passenger. When used to perform any tour service, the same vehicle is called a motorcoach.

C

CAA—(see Civil Aviation Authority)

CAB—(see Civil Aeronautics Board)

Cabana—A room in a beach or pool area, with or without beds, usually separate from a hotel's main building.

Cabin—A sleeping room on a ship; may imply less luxury than a stateroom. The passenger campartment of a plane.

Cabotage fare—A special rate within a political entity applicable to its nationals only on routes between two or more points. British Airways, for example, offers lower-than-IATA cabotage fares between many Commonwealth cities.

Cafe Complet—A mid-morning or afternoon snack with coffee; a frequent misnomer for Continental Breakfast.

CALPA—(see Canadian Air Line Pilots Association)

Cambio—An office where currencies may be exchanged. This Spanish word is used in many non-Spanish countries as well.

Canadian Air Line Pilots Association—A Canadian union affiliated with the International Association of Air Line Pilots Associations.

Canadian Air Traffic Control Association—A union of air traffic controllers that negotiates with the government all contract matters. The association is affiliated with the International Federation of Air Traffic Controllers Associations.

Canadian Government Office of Tourism—Official travel promotion agency of Canada.

Car and Truck Rental and Leasing Association—A trade group representing most major rental firms in the United States.

Caribbean Hotel Association—Affiliation of individual hotels and island hotel associations in the Caribbean and Bahamas as well as allied members providing related services.

Caribbean Tourism Association—A cooperative promotional agency supported by Caribbean national governments.

Carpati—Romanian national tourist organization.

Carriage—The act or process of transporting or carrying; the charge for transporting. As in passenger carriage, or freight carriage.

Carrier—Any organization that deals in transporting passengers or goods.

CATCA—(see Canadian Air Traffic Control Association)

Cathode Ray Tube (CRT)—A computer peripheral with a screen that allows a user to see what is being entered into the computer and to read the information the computer is sending to the user. They are the most frequently used terminals in automated reservation systems made available to agents. "Cathode ray" refers to a particular way in which light is projected on the screen, while a more generalized term for any TV-like screen used with computers is video display terminal.

CATM—(see Consolidated Air Tour Manual)

CATRALA—(see Car and Truck Rental and Leasing Association)

CEDOK—Czechoslovakian government travel organization.

CERR—(see Conference of European Railroad Representatives)

Certified Travel Counselor—A degree, usually abbreviated CTC, attesting to professional competence as a travel agent. It is conferred on completion of a course of study by the Institute of Certified Travel Agents. The Certified Travel Associate degree is awarded to non-agent personnel who have completed the course.

CF—Car Ferry.

CGOT—(see Canadian Government Office of Tourism)

CHA—(see Caribbean Hotel Association)

Charter—To hire the exclusive use of any aircraft, vessel or other vehicle.

Charter Airline—(see Supplemental)

Charter Boat—A vessel, usually used for fishing or sightseeing, available for hire on an exclusive basis.

Charter Flight—A flight booked exclusively for the use of a specific group or groups (see Split Charter) of people who belong generally to the same organization(s), or who are guests of a single host or who are traveling on an inclusive tour charter program. They may be carried out by scheduled or charter airlines. (see Public charter and Single Entity)

Check-in Time—Most hotel-days begin at 6 a.m., but an arriving guest may be unable to occupy his room until after the established check-out time, usually 1 p.m. An airline's check-in time is the time before the flight necessary for having passenger's ticket checked, luggage identified, x-raying, etc.

Check-Out Time—All hotels post a time (usually, but not necessarily, 1 p.m.) by which guests musuvacate their rooms. Late checkouts are often permitted but must be approved by the hotel management.

Child—In travel, the supplier defines the chronological limits of childhood. Fare structures and hotel rates often contain break-points at which children are offered reduced rates, but these vary. (see Airline Classes of Service, international and domestic fares)

Circle Fare—A special fare, lower than the sum of the point-to-point rates established for a circle trip.

Circle Trip—A journey with stopovers that returns to the point of departure without retracing its route. Travel from Point A with stops at Points B and C and returning to A is a circle trip, if Point B is off the regular route between Points A and C or Point C is off the regular route between Points A and B.

City Package—(see Package)

City Pair—The terminal communities in an air trip; the departure and destination points.

City Terminal—An airline ticket office, not located at an airport, where a passenger may check-in for a flight, check his baggage, receive his seat assignment and secure ground transportation to the airport.

City Ticket Office—A carrier ticket sales office or counter located outside a terminal.

Civil Aeronautics Board—The federal agency which regulates international air commerce to and from the U.S. and U.S. domestic air commerce. The CAB has authority to license air carriers and exercise control over their international routes and rates and their dealings with one another, other travel industry segments and the public. Safety is regulated by the Federal Aviation Administration. Under the Airline Deregulation Act of 1978, the CAB's powers are to be phased out or transferred to other government agencies by 1984.

Civil Aviation Authority—The agency which administers British civil aviation with responsibility for route licensing, safety standards and traffic control.

CLIA—(see Cruise Lines International Association)

Client—A travel agent's customer.

Coach Service—Air: U.S. domestic passenger carriage at the international equivalent of Economy.

Codes—(see Airline codes)

Co-Host Carrier—Any airline that concludes an agreement with an airline that is providing an automated reservation system to agents, whereby the co-host will pay part of the cost of providing improvements and arranging additional installations of the reservation system in agencies. In return, the co-host's flight listings and other pertinent data useful to agents get preferential treatment over other off-line carriers. The host and co-host often attempt other steps to increase the accuracy of information passed between them, leading in a few cases to direct computer-to-computer links.

Commercial Rate—A special rate agreed upon by a company (or other multi-purchaser) and a hotel or car rental firm. Usually, the hotel or car rental firm agree to supply rooms or cars of a specified quality or better at a flat rate.

Commission—The amount, which may vary, which a travel agent receives from the supplier for selling transportation, accommodations, or other services.

Common Carrier—Anyone or any organization which offers transport to all comers for hire.

Common Rated—Describing two or more relatively adjacent destinations for which the fare from a specific point of origin is identical.

Commuter Airline—Scheduled carrier unregulated by CAB, limited by law to small aircraft, and required to operate with 60 or fewer seats.

Companion Way—Stairs on a ship from one deck to another.

Concierge—In virtually all European hotels (and many elsewhere), the superintendent of minor services—porterage, mailing letters, making reservations and the like—for guests. The concierge is often a guest's principal link with both the hotel and the city in which it is located.

Conditions—The section or clause of a transportation or tour contract that specifies what is offered to the purchaser. A conditions clause often specifies what is **not** offered and may spell out the circumstances under which the contract may be invalidated in all or in part.

Conducted Tour—(see Escorted Tour)

Confederation of Latin-American Tourist Organizations—An association of national tourism promotional agencies.

Conference—An association of carriers formed to establish rules for the mutual benefit of its members. Among other things, a conference may establish rates; allocate routes; formulate and enforce safety, service and ethical standards; and establish rules governing the conduct of others (for example, travel agents) who do business with its members.

Conference of European Railroad Representatives—A professional association of New York City-based executives employed by European government railroads.

Confidential Tariff—A schedule of wholesale rates distributed in confidence to travel wholesalers and travel agents. (see Net Rate)

Configuration—The interior arrangement of a vehicle, particularly an airplane. The same aircraft, for example, might be configured for 190 Coach passengers; for 12 First Class passengers and 170 Coach passengers; for 12 First Class passengers, 100 Coach passengers and two cargo pallets; or for any other combination within its capacity.

Confirmed Reservation—An oral or written statement by a supplier (a carrier, hotel, car rental company, etc.) that he has received and will honor a reservation. Oral confirmations have virtually no legal worth. Even written or telegraphed confirmations have specified or implied limitations. For example, a hotel is not obligated to honor a reservation if the guest

176

arrives after 6 p.m., unless late arrival is specified. However, if the reservation is guaranteed, then that hotel is obligated to honor it.

Conjunction Tickets—Two or more air tickets, concurrently issued, which together constitute a single contract of carriage.

Connecting Flight—A segment of an ongoing journey which requires passengers to change aircraft (but not necessarily carriers). Under IATA regulations, a flight connection becomes a stopover if the passenger is required to wait more than 24 hours for his next flight.

Connecting Rooms—Two or more rooms with private doors permitting access from one to the other without use of hotel corridor.

Connecting Time—(see Minimum Connecting Time)

ConRail—The name under which the Consolidated Rail Corp. operates primarily freight rail service in the Northeast. It was established as a private corporation by Congress to take over and operate facilities formerly owned by Penn Central and five other bankrupt railroads. It is not corporately linked with Amtrak.

Consolidated Air Tour Manual—A trade catalogue of tours and packages published annually by 18 U.S. and Canadian airlines in three editions—all-year, winter and spring-summer-fall. Covers all U.S. destinations, the Bahamas, Mexico, Canada and the Caribbean.

Consolidation—Cancellation by a charter tour operator of one or more flights associated with a specific charter departure or departure period with the transfer of passengers to another charter flight or flights to depart on or near the same day. Selling the same tour with identical departure dates through a number of wholesalers, cooperatives or other outlets in order to increase sales and reduce the possibility of tour cancellations.

Consolidator—A person or company which forms groups to travel on air charters or at group fares on scheduled flights to increase sales, earn override commissions or reduce the possibility of tour cancellations.

Continental Breakfast—At a minimum, a beverage (coffee, tea or milk) and rolls or toast. Sometimes includes fruit juice. In Holland and Norway, may include cheese, meat or fish.

Continental Plan—A hotel rate that includes bed and continental breakfast.

Contractor—A land operator which provides services to wholesalers, tour operators and travel agents.

COTAL—(see Confederation of Latin-American Tourist Organizations)

Council on International Student Exchange—A non-profit organization which encourages and facilitates travel and study in foreign countries by students.

Counter Agent—A carrier ticket agent.

Coupon, Flight—The portion of a passenger ticket that indicates the route on which passage has been purchased.

Coupon, Passenger—The portion of an airline ticket that constitutes written evidence to the passenger of the contract of carriage.

Coupon, Tour—(see Voucher)

CP—(see Continental Plan)

Creative—Indicates the production of new business, particularly for airlines. A creative travel agent presumably produces new business by inducing people to travel. Airline marketing men believe that agents who produce a high percentage of pleasure and group sales are more creative than those who produce business and point-to-point sales.

Cruise—A sea voyage for pleasure (as opposed to one for transportation) which usually—but not always—returns to its departure point.

Cruise Lines International Association (CLIA)—An organization formed to promote cruising as an entity, conduct educational programs on cruising for agency staff and management, and to provide a forum for discussion among shiplines.

CTA—(see Caribbean Travel Association)

CTA—Certified Travel Associate. (see Certified Travel Counselor)

CTC—(see Certified Travel Counselor)

CTO—(see City Ticket Office)

CTRC—Caribbean Tourism Research Centre.

Currency, Basic—IATA air fares are expressed either in U.S. dollars or British pounds sterling depending on the area or areas in which they are applicable as follows: Dollars are used within Area I and between Areas 1 and 2 and between Areas 1 and 3, Sterling is used within and between Areas 2 and 3. The industry is now utilizing Fare Construction Units or FCU for basing fares. An FCU is first established and then all currencies are related to it. Strong currencies end up lower than the FCU and weaker currencies higher.

D

Data Retrieval System or Fact File—A collection of general travel-related information prepared and filed in a reservation system by a host carrier for retrieval by agents as needed. It can include everything from the host carrier's newest fare filings to current theater offerings at various destinations, plus more static information like visa or document requirements and currency information for various destinations and descriptions of ground transportation and hotels at various cities, etc.

Day-Rate—A special rate for non-overnight use of a hotel room. Usually good only between 6 a.m. and 5 p.m.

DBA—Doing business as…For example, the Doe Travel Co. might do business as Doe Travel Tours. Thus, Doe Travel Co., dba Doe Travel Tours.

Deadhead—Noun: A person traveling on a free pass, more specifically an airline crew or crew member in transit; any aircraft, ship or vehicle in transit without a payload. Verb: To operate any empty vehicle. (see Ferry Flight)

Deck—"Floor" on a ship.

Deltamatic—Delta's reservation system.

Deluxe—In travel usage, presumably "of the highest standard." A much misused and, in many respects, meaningless term except where employed as part of an official rating system. (see Hotel Classifications)

Demi-Pension—A hotel rate including bed, breakfast and either lunch or dinner. MAP.

Denied Boarding Compensation—The prescribed penalty paid to a passenger in the event that an airline fails to honor a confirmed reservation because of overbooking.

Department of Transportation—The U.S. federal agency, headed by a member of the President's Cabinet, charged with developing and implementing policies designed to improve and regulate all domestic and international transportation facilities and organizations. By law, however, some federal transportation agencies (such as the CAB) operate outside the jurisdiction of the Secretary of Transportation.

Departure Tax—(see head Tax)

Deposit Reservation—A reservation for which the hotel has received cash payment for at least one night's lodging in advance and is obligated to hold the room regardless of the guest's arrival. Most commercial hotels do not feel obligated to refund deposits unless reservations are cancelled at least 48 hours in advance. Cancellation policies at resort hotels vary and should be verified in advance.

Destination—The place to which a traveler is going. In the travel industry: any city, area or country which can be marketed as a single entity to tourists.

Diner—A railroad restaurant car.

Direct Air Carrier—An air carrier, generally applied only to one operating charter flights.

Direct Flight—A journey on which the passenger does not have to change planes. Not necessarily non-stop.

Directional Tariff—A reduced fare—often seasonal and usually round-trip—offered passengers originating at one end of a route only. A Westbound Transatlantic Directional tariff would offer passengers originating in Europe a lower rate than that offered passengers originating in North America.

Discriminatory—In reference to fares: Offering lower rates to certain people—servicemen, young people, old people, etc. Such promotional fares are under constant—and sometimes successful—attack on grounds that they are unfair to those ineligible to use them.

DIT—Domestic independent travel. A prepaid, unescorted tour within a country designed to the specifications of an individual client or clients.

Dome Car—(see Observation Car)

DOT—(see Department of Transportation)

Double—Loosely, any hotel room for two persons; more specifically, a room with a double bed. A room with two smaller beds is a twin.

Double-Double—(see Twin Double)

Double-Occupancy Rate—The price **per person** for a room to be shared with another person. The rate most frequently quoted in tour brochures.

Double Room Rate—The full price of a room for two people, but be careful: Some people say double when they mean double occupancy.

Downgrade—To move to a lesser accommodation or class of service.

DP—(see Demi-Pension)

Dry Lease—The rental of a vehicle, particularly an aircraft, without an operator or crew. A pure dry lease would be without supplies, fuel or maintenance service. (See Wet Lease)

DSM—District Sales Manager.

Duplex—A two-story suite connected by a private stairway.

E

ECAC—(see European Civil Aviation Conference)

Economy Fare or Service—In U.S. domestic airline operations: Passenger carriage at a level below Coach service. In international operations: Carriage at a level below First Class.

Economy Hotel—(see Hotel Classification)

Efficiency—Any accommodation containing some sort of cooking facilities.

English Breakfast—Generally served in the U.K. and Ireland. Usually includes fruit or fruit juice; hot or cold cereal; bacon, ham, sausages or kippers; eggs; toast; butter; jam or marmalade, and tea or coffee.

Entry Tax (or Fee)—(see Head Tax)

EP—(see European Plan)

Escorted Tour—(1) A prearranged travel program, usually for a group, with escort service. Fully-escorted tours may have escorts throughout plus local guide service in some areas. (2) A sightseeing program conducted by a guide.

Escrow Accounts—Funds placed in the custody of licensed financial institutions for safe-keeping. Many contracts in travel require that agents and tour operators maintain customers deposits and prepayments in escrow accounts.

ETC—(see European Travel Commission)

Eurailpass—A European railroad pass sold overseas for a flat rate for a specified number of days. It provides unlimited First Class travel through 15 European countries. Also available at student and children's rates.

European Civil Aviation Conference—An association concerned with facilitating air commerce within Europe. Nations are represented by their civil aviation directors.

European Plan—A hotel rate that includes bed only; any meals are extra.

European Travel Commission—A cooperative agency sponsored by Western European governments for the promotion of tourism.

Excess Baggage—Baggage in excess of specified size or weight by the particular carrier.

Exchange Order—A document issued by a carrier or its agent requesting issue of a ticket or provision of other specified services to the person named in the document.

Excursion—A journey, usually short, made with the intention of returning to the starting point.

Excursion Fare—Any fare offering roundtrip transportation below the combined cost of the component one-way fares.

Extension—A fully-arranged sub-tour offered optionally at extra cost to buyers of a tour or cruise. Extensions may occur before, during or after the basic travel program.

F

FAA—(see Federal Aviation Administration)

Familiarization Tour—A complimentary of reduced-rate travel program for travel agents and/or airline employees that is designed to acquaint them with specific destination or destinations to stimulate the sale of travel.

Family Motor Coach Association—Association of house trailer and motorhome owners.

Family Plan—A discount schedule offered by hotels and resorts, to second and successive members of families who travel together.

Fan Jet—(see Turbofan Jet)

Fantail—The stern overhang of a ship.

180

Fares—

Add On—the amount of fare arbitrarily added onto an international fare to reach an inland point, i.e., there is an add on to cover the cost between New York and Salt Lake City for a trip between Europe and Salt Lake City.

All Year—Not limited by a ticket validity of less than one year.

Basic—A specified or constructed fare expressed in U.S. dollars or British pounds depending on the IATA area or areas to which they apply. (see Currency, Basic)

Combined—Obtained by comining two or more fares not published as a single amount.

Combination Joint—A joint fare obtained by combining two or more published fares.

Constructed—Established in accordance with an applicable IATA Traffic Conference resolution or resolutions. On a complicated itinerary, skillful fare construction can often produce significant rate reductions.

Interline or Joint—Applying to carriage over routes of two more carriers and published as a single amount.

Normal—The full established peak-season rate.

Proportional—For use only in combination with other rates for carriage to, from or through a specified point.

Special—As established in an applicable IATA Traffic Conference resolution.

Specified—As established in an applicable IATA Traffic Conference resolution.

Through—From point of departure to point of destination; either a joint fare or a combination of fares.

Federal Aviation Administration—The Department of Transportation agency that regulates U.S. civil aviation. Among other things, FAA licenses private and commercial pilots; certifies aircraft and monitors their maintenance; certifies and monitors airport traffic control systems and their personnel, and enforces airline security regulations.

Federal Maritime Administration—A unit of the U.S. Transportation Department which administers federal programs affecting water-borne commerce, the Merchant Marine and the American shipbuilding industry. It also administers federal subsidy programs for American passenger and cargo ships.

Federal Maritime Commission—The U.S. federal regulatory agency with authority over international passenger and cargo carriage.

Federation of International Youth Travel Organizations—A worldwide association promoting travel for students and young people.

Ferry Flight—The non-revenue positioning flight of an empty aircraft, usually in charter service. (see Deadhead)

FET—Foreign escorted tour.

FGTO—French Government Tourist Office, the official French agency for the promotion of tourism.

FIAV—Italian Federation of Travel Agents.

FIJET—International Federation of Travel Editors and Writers.

Final Itinerary—(see Itinerary)

First Class Fare or Service—In air, rail and sea travel, the best and most expensive way to go. (see Airline and Railroad Classes of Service)

First Class Hotel—An average, comfortable hotel. (see Hotel Classifications)

First Refusal Rights—A pre-emptive government policy of allowing a favored carrier or class of carrier to claim and operate revenue charter flights planned by other airlines. Some governments, for example, do not allow charter airlines of other countries to operate in their territory unless certain other airlines are given the option of operating the charter.

FIT—Foreign independent travel. An international, prepaid tour, usually unescorted although guide service is often offered on some segments. An FIT is designed to the specifications of an individual client or clients.

FIT Operator (or **Wholesaler**)—A specialist in preparing and operating FITs at the request of retail travel agents.

FIYTO—(see Federation of International Youth Travel Organizations)

Flag Carrier—Any carrier designated by its government to operate international services.

Flag-Stop—A point on a scheduled train or airline route at which the carrier stops to pick up or discharge passengers only on signal.

Flight—A scheduled air service, identified by a flight number, from departure point through any designated stops to destination point and operated as a single entity.

Flume Stabilizer—(see Stabilizer)

Flyer—A printed advertisement intended for distribution to potential customers, usually by mail.

FMC—(see Federal Maritime Commission)

Folder—Any travel supplier's printed advertisement. Technically, a folder is not a brochure.

Fore (Forward)—In or toward the bow of a vessel.

Four Corners Regional Organization—Joint travel promotion by the states of Arizona, Colorado, New Mexico and Utah, using tour packaging and other means to promote the region under the umbrella name of The Four Most West.

Four Most West—(see Four Corners Regional Organization)

FP—(see Full Pension)

France-Congres—An association formed by mayors of several French cities which functions as a national convention bureau for France.

Freedoms of the Air—A concept never agreed upon between countries that there should be six "freedoms" of air commerce. The six freedoms, in order, are: (1) The right of an aircraft of one country to fly across the territory of another nation without landing, (2) right of that aircraft to land for non-traffic purposes, (3) right of an airline of one nation to disembark in a second country traffic originating in its home country, (4) right of an airline of one nation to pick up in another country traffic destined for the country of the airline's nationality, (5) right of an airline to carry traffic from a point of origin in one foreign country to a point of destination in another foreign country and (6) right of an airline to carry traffic from a foreign country to the home nation of that airline and beyond to another foreign country.

Free Sale—The practice of permitting the confirmation of a specified number of reservations (within specified dates) without reference to the principal for confirmation.

Full Pension—Particularly in Europe, a hotel rate that includes three meals daily; an American Plan rate.

Fully Appointed—Refers to a travel agent who has received official recognition from the major airline, steamship and railroad conferences. (see Appointment)

G

Gap—In reference to an airline itinerary: that portion of the trip involving transportation by means other than an IATA or ATA airline.

Garni—As applied to European hotels: without restaurant services except for continental breakfast.

Gateway—City, airport or area from which a flight or tour departs.

General Sales Agent—An agency or another airline named by an airline as its sales agent in a specific country or territory. TWA, for example, is general sales agent in the United States for Kenya Airways.

GIANTS—(see Greater Independent Association of National Travel Services)

GIT—(see Group Inclusive Tour)

182

GMT—(see Greenwich Mean Time)

Go-Show—(see Standby Passenger)

Greater Independent Association of National Travel Services—A sales and marketing cooperative of retail travel agents.

Greenwich Mean Time—The mean solar time at Greenwich, England, used as the basis for calculating time throughout the world.

Gross Register Ton—100 cubic feet of enclosed space on a ship; passenger ship sizes are expressed in gross register tons. (see Tonnage)

Ground Arrangements—(see Land Arrangements)

Ground Operator—(see Land Operator)

Group Inclusive Tour—A prepaid tour of specified minimum size, ingredients and value. (see GIT Fare)

GSA—(see General Sales Agent)

Guaranteed Payment Reservation—A hotel reservation secured by the guest's agreement to pay for his room whether he uses it or not. Payment is usually guaranteed by a company, travel agent or tour wholesaler who has an established credit rating with the hotel or use a credit card as a guarantee.

Guaranteed Tour—A tour guaranteed to operate unless cancelled before an established cutoff date (usually 60 days prior to departure).

Guest-Night—(see Bed-Night)

Guide—(1) A person qualified to conduct tours of specific localities or attractions. Many reliable guides are licensed. (2) An airline, bus, railroad or ship manual of schedules and fares. Listings are not guaranteed, but travel agents and carrier reservationists use such manuals as a matter of necessity.

Guided Tour—A local sightseeing trip conducted by a guide.

Gyro-Stabilizer—(see Stabilizer)

H

Half Pension—(see Demi-Pension)

Half-roundtrip—Half of an air charter roundtrip sold as a roundtrip but priced in halves because the two halves may be taken in different seasonal pricing periods. Since the return trip on the same carrier is assured, the half-roundtrip is generally priced somewhat lower than a one-way fare.

Head Tax—A fee collected from a passenger as a prerequisite for his departure from or entry into a city or country.

Hire Car—British and European for rental automobile, with or without driver.

Hospitality—Hotel room used for entertaining, usually a function room or parlor.

Hospitality Suite—A hotel suite, parlor or studio engaged for the entertainment of those attending a convention or similar meeting.

Host—(1) A representative of the tour operator, destination or other tour principal who provides escort service at the destination. The term *host-escort* is often used to make a distinction between this function and (2) such representatives who provide only information or greeting services or who assist at the destination with ground arrangements without actually accompanying the tour.

Host Carrier—The airline with which the agent user of an automated reservation system is communicating directly. Usually the host carrier is the airline that is marketing its own computerized system to agents, but the term applies to any airline participant in a multi-access system at the time the agency is communicating directly with its computer to make reservations.

Hostel—An inexpensive, supervised lodging, particularly for young people.

Hostelry—An inn; by extension, any accommodation that provides food and/or lodging to travelers.

Host-Escort—(See Host)

Hotel Classification—The following designations are generally understood throughout Europe and, to an extent, the world, but it is sometimes difficult to know whether a hotel is being described by a reliable source or at the whim of a promoter. There is neither an official nor generally-accepted rating system for U.S. hotels.

Deluxe—A top-grade hotel; all rooms have private bath; all the usual public rooms and services are provided; a high standard of decor and services is maintained.

First Class—A medium-range hotel; at least some rooms have private bath; most of the usual public rooms and services are provided.

Tourist (Economy or Second Class)—Budget operations; few or no private baths; services may be very limited.
The Official Hotel & Resort Guide further subdivides these three categories into three groups; superior, average and moderate. Thus, a superior, deluxe hotel rates with the best in the world and an average, first class hotel is about in mid-range. OHRG says that hotels below its superior tourist rating should be used with caution by Westerners.
In addition, many governments rate their hotels according to the international five-star system under which a five star hotel is the best. Some countries are meticulous and generally current in their ratings; many are not. In general, three star and better hotels (and a few two-star properties) are believed suitable for Western travelers.

Hotel & Travel Index—A Ziff-Davis quarterly directory covering rates, commission rates, capacity, services, location and representation of more than **33,000** hotels and resorts throughout the world.

Hotelier—A hotel-keeper.

Hotel Package—(see Package) A package offered by a hotel, sometimes consisting of no more than a room and breakfast, and other times, especially at resort hotels, of transportation, room, meals, sports facilities and other components.

Hotel Register—The permanent record maintained by all hotels of the arrival and departure of guests, all of whom must sign it on arrival.

Hotel Rep or Representative—A person (or company) who offers hotel reservations to wholesalers, travel agents and the public. He is paid by the hotels he represents on a fee basis. Many hotel reps also offer marketing and other services.

Hotel Sales Management Association—A professional society.

Housing Bureau—An organization, often government-sponsored, which acts as a clearing house for accommodations, particularly for conventions and other large meetings. Often established on an ad hoc basis during major touristic events to maintain a registry of private accommodations to supplement an area's regular lodging industry.

HSMA—(see Hotel Sales Management Association)

HTI—(see Hotel & Travel Index)

I

IACA—(see International Air Carrier Association)

IAMAT—(see International Association for Medical Assistance to Travelers)

IATA—(see International Air Transport Association)

IATAS—(see Inter-American Travel Agents Society)

IATC—(see Inter-American Travel Congress)

IATM—(see International Association of Tour Managers)

ICAO—(see International Civil Aviation Organization)

ICC—(see Interstate Commerce Commission)

ICCA—(see International Congress and Convention Association)

ICTA—(see Institute of Certified Travel Agents)

IDB—(see Inter-American Development Bank)

IHA—(see International Hotel Association)

Inaugural—Under IATA rules a carrier may designate any single flight on a new route or with new equipment within 6 months of the actual inaugural as the inaugural flight. On such flights, carriers may invite guests and, if they wish, pay for their ground arrangements.

Incentive, or Incentive Commission—(see Override)

Incentive Travel—(1) A trip offered as a prize, particularly to stimulate the productivity of employees or sales agents; (2) The business of operating such travel programs.

Inclusive Tour—A tour in which specific elements—air fare, hotels, transfers, etc.—are offered for a flat rate. An inclusive tour rate does not necessarily cover all costs. (see All Expense Tour)

Indirect Air Carrier—Generally synonymous with charter tour operator. A tour operator, travel agent or other promoter who, under CAB regulations, contracts for charter space from an airline for resale to the public. In theory, indirect air carriers act as independent, risk-taking entrepreneurs, promoting their own product, rather than as agents of the airline.

Infrastructure—Loosely, anything that supports travel. Legally, the government and quasi-governmental machinery that regulates and/or promotes travel and related industries. Physically, in a developing area, the public utilities—highways, water supply, electric power, etc.—needed to support a tourist plant. In a developed area, the entire local transportation, lodging, restaurant, entertainment and cultural establishment.

In-Plant Agency—A travel agent's sales outlet located on the premises of a company and confined to doing business for that company only. In-plant air commissions are lower than those paid regularly; at this writing, only a handful of agents maintained in-plant locations.

Institute of Certified Travel Agents—An organization concerned with developing and administering educational programs for travel agents. (see CTC)

Inter-American Development Bank—A lending institution sponsored by the U.S. and other governments charged with financing industries (including those related to tourism) in underdeveloped Western Hemisphere nations.

Inter-American Travel Agents Society—A trade association of black travel agents.

Interface—In the travel agency business, a direct link between an airline reservation system and the agency's in-house computer which allows the capture of all pertinent data from each airline booking for various bookkeeping purposes and for use in appropriate business reports. Without the link, the agency staff would have to enter all data pertaining to bookings into computers twice, once to make the reservation and later for accounting purposes. In most arrangements, the agency's own printers also print airline tickets and itineraries/invoices, replacing the service that can be provided by printers made available by the reservation system vendor.

Interliner—(1) An airline employee traveling on another airline. (2) An airline reservationist who arranges transportation for passengers on a carrier(s) other than his own.

Interline Rep—An airline salesman who deals with other airlines.

International Air Carrier Association—A trade association of charter airlines based in Brussels, which operate internationally. The group allows scheduled airlines to join as associate members.

International Air Transport Association—The world trade association of airlines which operate domestic and international services. IATA operates as a supra-national organization, proposing rates, conditions of service, safety standards, etc., and provides the machinery which makes the unified world system of air transportation possible.

International Association of Amusement Parks and Attractions—An association of theme parks, amusement parks, zoos, resorts and other recreational facilities.

International Association for Medical Assistance to Travelers—A non-profit organization which maintains a worldwide registry of physicians who speak English and have taken medical training in the U.S., the U.K. or Canada.

International Association of Tour Managers—A professional society of tour escorts.

International Civil Aviation Organization—An organization of governments which works in relationship with the United Nations to promote the safety of international civil aviation by standardizing technical equipment, services and training. ICAO also provides economic and statistical services to airlines and governments and extends technical assistance to developing countries.

International Congress and Convention Association—A European-based trade association.

International Date Line—An imaginary line in the Pacific Ocean roughly at 180 degrees longitude where, by international agreement, the earth's day begins. Eastbound passengers crossing the date line gain a day, i.e. Tuesday becomes Monday. Westbound passengers lose a day.

International Hotel Association—A European-based trade association.

International Passenger Ship Association—A trade association of shiplines which operate cruises marketed in North America. As the successor to the Atlantic Passenger Ship Association, IPSA appoints travel agents to sell the vast majority of cruises offered in North America.

International Sightseeing and Tours Association—A European-based trade association of sightseeing operators.

International Student Identity Card—A document issued by the Council of International Student Exchange to qualified students. A student card will often help the bearer to secure special travel rates and other benefits.

Interstate Commerce Commission—An independent regulatory agency created by Congress to regulate surface transportation by common carriers, such as railroads, bus companies and pipeline operators. With regard to travel, it regulates the rates and routes of the scheduled bus companies.

Intourist—USSR government agency for foreign travel.

ISTA—(see International Sightseeing and Tours Association)

IT—(see Inclusive tour)

IT Number—The code designation on an inclusive tour folder indicating that the tour has been approved by ATC or IATA. Agents who sell such tours qualify for override commissions on air tickets sold in connection with them.

Itinerary—The travel schedule provided by a travel agent for his client. A proposed or preliminary itinerary may be rather vague or very specific. A final itinerary, however, spells out all details—flight numbers, departure times, etc.—as well as describing planned activities. It should be delivered shortly before departure.

ITX—Inclusive Tour Excursion. British and Continental usage for an inclusive tour fare.

IUOTO—The International Union of Official Travel Organizations, now known as the World Tourism Organization.

J, K

Japan Association of Travel Agents—A trade association in Japan.

JATA—(see Japan Association of Travel Agents)

JATO—Jet assisted take-off, a system which provides extra power during take-offs of aircraft powered by piston engines.

JaxFax—A directory of charter flights and group departures on scheduled flights published by Jet Airtransport Exchange, Inc.

Jet—Any aircraft powered by turbo-jet engines.

Jitney—A small bus or automobile that serves a route on a more or less flexible schedule.

Jones Act—A law first passed by Congress in 1886 barring ships of foreign registry from transporting passengers between U.S. ports. As now interpreted by the Customs Service, it allows foreign cruise ships to move between two U.S. ports under certain circumstances.

JNTO—Japan National Tourist Organization, the official Japanese agency for the promotion of tourism.

Junior Suite—A large hotel room with a partition separating the bedroom and sitting area.

Knot—A unit of speed, one nautical mile per hour, about 1.15 statute miles per hour.

L

Lanai—Generally, a veranda. In travel, a room with a balcony or patio overlooking water or a garden, usually in a resort hotel.

Land Arrangements—All services provided to a client (except ongoing transportation by public carrier) after he has reached destination.

Land Operator—A company that provides local travel services, transfers, sightseeing, guides, etc.

Leg—The portion of flight between any two consecutive scheduled stops.

Lido Deck—The area on a ship around a swimming pool; on some ships the entire deck on which the pool is located.

Limousine—A large chauffeur-driven sedan. Usually for transporting guests between airports and hotels.

Load Factor—The ratio, expressed as a percentage, of carrier capacity sold to total capacity offered for sale. If a 100-seat aircraft carries 75 paying passengers, that flight is operated at a 75% load factor. If an airline operates 100,000 seat miles and its sales total 50,000 revenue passenger miles, it is operating at a 50% load factor.

Local Operator—(see Land Operator)

Lower—A berth on a ship or train that is beneath another. (see Railroad Classes of Service)

Low Season—That time of the year at any given destination when tourist traffic (and often rates) is at its lowest.

MAA—(see Motel Association of America)

Manifest—A document listing all the passengers and/or describing all the cargo on an airline flight or other trip by common carrier.

Manual—Any compendium of tariffs and/or schedules of carriers, hotels, sightseeing services, etc.

MAP—(see Modified American Plan)

MCO—(see Miscellaneous Charges Order)

Meditercongress—International Association of Organizations and Congress Cities of the States Interested in the Mediterranean Area.

Meetings & Conventions—A Ziff-Davis monthly trade publication for executives concerned with conventions, meetings and incentive travel programs.

Minimum Connecting Time—The time, separately established for every commercial airport, required to leave one scheduled flight and board another. A passenger ticketed with less than the published minimum connecting time has no recourse (except to complain to whoever issued the ticket) if he fails to make his connection. If the proper minimum has been observed, the delivering airline is responsible for a failure to connect and must provide an onward flight and/or meals and lodging as necessary. Receiving airlines are not obligated to wait for connecting passengers but at times may do so.

Minimum Land Package—The minimum, expressed in terms of cost and ingredients, tour that must be purchased to qualify a passenger for an airline inclusive tour, group inclusive tour or contract bulk inclusive tour fare. Such packages usually must include a certain number of nights lodging, other specified ingredients such as sightseeing and/or entertainment and/or car rental. The minimum rate for the combined air fares and ground package is often expressed as a percentage (often 100% or 110%) of the lowest regular fare for the air travel scheduled.

Miscellaneous Charges Order—A document issued by an airline or its agent requesting the issue of a ticket or provision of services to the person named in the order.

Modem—A device used to convert computer electronic pulses into audio tones so information can be carried between two computers over telephone lines. Travel agencies with automated reservation systems have these small black boxes in their offices so their CRTs can communicate with the airline computer some distance away.

Modified American Plan—A hotel room rate including breakfast and either lunch or dinner.

Mom and Pop Shop—A small travel agency operated by a husband and wife. By extension: Any independently owned small agency.

Motel Association of America—A confederation of state trade associations of motel operators located in the continental U.S.

Motorcoach—A large highway passenger vehicle used to perform any travel service other than scheduled transportation for individually-ticketed passengers. (see Bus)

MS—Motor Ship.

MTS—Motor Turbine Ship.

Multi-Access Reservations System—A computerized reservation package that is provided by an airline or non-airline vendor, but which provides agency users with direct access to the computers of several airlines and any other travel suppliers that are willing to be participants. The computers of participating airlines can then be used to book space on non-participating airlines, hotels, car rental firms, etc.

MV—Motor Vessel.

N

NACA—(see National Air Carrier Association)

NARP—(see National Association of Railroad Passengers)

NATC—(see National Air Transport Conference)

National Air Carrier Association—The trade association of U.S. supplemental airlines.

National Air Transportation Association—A group representing air-taxi and other small aircraft operators and aviation service companies (such as fuel, maintenance and leasing firms).

National Association of Railroad Passengers—A lobby group promoting the preservation and growth of rail travel.

National Passenger Traffic Association—The trade group representing corporate travel managers.

National Tour Association—A trade association of U.S. motorcoach tour operators.

National Transportation Safety Board—The agency that develops safety standards for all modes of public transportation and investigates accidents. (see FAA)

Need/Need—A message used by agents with computerized reservation systems when booking space with an off-line carrier. The purpose is to make sure a seat is available when there is reason to doubt the information in the host carrier's computer. The need/need message forces the host carrier to send a message to the second line and forces the second line to confirm a specific seat for the agency client and to send a message back to the first airline. Ordinarily, the host line simply confirms a second carrier's space to the agent from a small standing inventory and informs the off-line carrier later. (See Sell/Sell)

Net Rate—A wholesale rate to be marked up for eventual resale to the consumer. (see Confidential Tariff)

No Go—A flight that will not be operated.

No Rec—Shorthand for no record, referring to situations when passenger name records seemingly get lost when being transferred from one carrier to another. Usually the message has for some reason been rejected by the second carrier's computer and gone to a separate file for handling manually. This sometimes takes too long, which means a client may show up at the airport and find that the second carrier shows no record of the booking. In other words, so-called no recs are usually really slow-recs, or slow records.

Non Revenue or Non Rev—A flight on which no paying passengers are carried or a passenger, usually an airline employee, who has not paid for a ticket.

Non-Sked—Non-scheduled.

Non-Stop Flight—Service between two points with no scheduled traffic stops en route. (see Direct Flight)

No Show—(1) A passenger or guest who fails either to use or cancel his reservation. (2) A reservation neither cancelled nor fulfilled.

NPTA—(see National Passenger Traffic Association)

NTA—(see National Tour Association)

NTSB—(see National Transportation Safety Board)

NYTWA—New York Travel Writers Association.

O

OAG—(see Official Airline Guide)

Observation Car—Any railroad car on which special provisions have been made for sightseeing. The original observation cars merely offered a sort of open back porch; some observation cars have high windows that curve into the roof, others (Bubble or Dome cars) have upper decks with glass roofs; many have special seats that swivel to face in any direction.

Occupancy Rate—The ratio, expressed as a percentage, of bed nights sold to the total offered for sale, by a hotel or group of hotels.

Offering—Any advertised tour or package.

Official Airline Guide—Any of the several passenger and cargo air service manuals in general use throughout the world. There are two principal passenger OAGs—the North American and Worldwide editions.

Official Hotel and Resort Guide—A Ziff-Davis directory which describes and rates **30,000** hotels, resorts and motor hotels throughout the world. The OHRG is published in a loose-leaf format to permit both regular and extraordinary revisions on a continuous basis.

Official Meeting Facilities Guide—A Ziff-Davis semi-annual directory covering rates, accommodations, meeting capacities and available services and equipment at resorts and hotels throughout the world.

Off-Line—Describes any carrier employee, facility or function located or performed at a point off that carrier's route structure. Thus: off line sales rep, off line ticket office, off line agency, etc.

Off-Line Carrier Any airline other than the one whose computer an automated agency is using to get information and make reservations. More generally, the term off-line also refers to any carrier other than the airline the agency is using to make a booking involving several airlines, even if the reservation is made by telephone.

Off-Peak—In reference to a fare or a hotel rate, other than the period(s) that are usually busiest.

Off-Route Charter—A flight by a scheduled airline to or from a point which it is not authorized to serve on a regularly scheduled basis. Some governments put limits on the number and/or frequency of off-route charters.

OHRG—(see Official Hotel and Resort Guide)

OMFG—(see Official Meeting Facilities Guide)

One-way—In reference to any fare, the rate for transportation from one point to another, without provision for a return journey.

On-Route Charter—A charter flight by a scheduled airline between points which it is authorized to serve on a regularly scheduled basis.

Open Jaw—(1) Referring to a roundtrip or roundtrip ticket on which (a) the point of outward departure is separated from the inward point of arrival, or (b) the point of outward arrival is separated from the inward point of departure, or (c) both outward and inward points of arrival and departure are separated. (2) The segment of an open jaw trip for which no transportation is provided. From New York to San Francisco with a return from Los Angeles is an open jaw.

Open Rate—Refers to a situation in which the IATA airlines have failed to negotiate uniform rate on certain routes leaving each carrier free to set its own rates.

Open Ticket—A ticket which does not specify when a service is to be performed, leaving the passenger responsible for securing a reservation (subject to availability) at a later date.

Operator—A loose term that may mean contractor, tour operator or wholesaler (see main listings) or a combination of any or all of those functions.

Option—A tour extension or sidetrip offered at extra cost.

Orbis—Polish National Travel Bureau.

Other Service Indicated—A piece of information that is included in a client's airline booking record but which does not necessarily require specified action by the carrier providing transportation. For example, an agent may simply ask that the line do "all possible" to make a VIP customer happy.

Overbooking—(1) The practice by a supplier of confirming reservations beyond capacity in expectation of cancellations or no shows. (2) The same occurrence due to error. (3) Any occurrence brought about due to lack of space. Many carriers have admitted that they intentionally overbook their flights because of the high number of passengers who are no shows. Various governments are insisting that carriers take steps to make this practice more widely known to passengers.

Override—An extra commission; sometimes called an overriding commission. Airlines pay overrides on ticket sales made in conjunction with tour sales and during the current un-regulated commission situation in the U.S. overrides are being paid for volume bookings. Wholesalers pay them as bonuses for volume business. Suppliers pay them to provide a profit margin for wholesalers (who must themselves pay commissions). Hotel groups or governments pay them as a volume incentive to wholesalers.

Oversale—A situation in which the expected no shows appear at the gate demanding space that does not exist. At this point, the flight is not merely overbooked, but oversold, and the extra passengers "bumped." (see Overbooking)
U.S. domestic carriers and international carriers serving the United States have varying regulations as to what services must be provided to bumped passengers and the affected passengers may demand to be shown copies of these regulations and be provided with the specified services.

P, Q

Pacific Area Travel Association—An organization of nations interested in promoting tourism throughout the Pacific and Indian Ocean areas.

Package—Loosely, any advertised tour. Often, however, a tour to a single destination which includes prepaid transportation, accommodations and some combination of other tour elements—meals, transfers, sightseeing, car rental, etc. A package may include more than one destination—for example, a cruise—but the term connotes an offering intended to provide a holiday rather than meet the cultural or other requirements of the more serious traveler.

Packager—Anyone who organizes and advertises a tour or a package; a wholesaler.

Package Tour—(see Package)

Parlor—A living or sitting room not used as a bedroom. In some parts of Europe, called a salon.

PARS—TWA's reservation system.

Part Charter—A charter concept under which a scheduled airline would transport charter passengers on regularly-scheduled flights, as a fill-up or cost-saving device. Although the CAB has never authorized part charters per se, it has allowed marketing devices which are, for all practical purposes, nearly identical—the bulk fare, for example.

Passenger—Strictly speaking, any person that any carrier is transporting or has agreed to transport; often used, however with the connotation of "paying passenger."

Passenger Mile—One passenger carried one mile. (see Revenue Passenger Mile)

Passenger Name Record (PNR)—The record of a booking made and stored in a computerized reservation system. It includes all the pertinent information about the reservation such as name of passenger, flight number, travel times, dates of travel, airline to be used, cost of ticket, etc. It could be the record of a non-air booking as well.

Passenger, Through—A passenger continuing his journey on the same scheduled aircraft, bus, ship or train.

Passenger, Transfer—A transit passenger scheduled to change vehicles.

Passenger, Transit—A passenger scheduled to continue his journey without a stopover. More specifically, a passenger who has left his aircraft (or other vehicle) during a stop; he may be either a through or a transfer passenger.

Passenger Traffic Manager—An employee who makes travel arrangements for other employees of his company.

Passport—An official government document that certifies the identity and citizenship of an individual and grants him permission to travel abroad.

PATA—(see Pacific Area Travel Association)

Peak Fare, Rate or Season—On many carriers and at many destinations, the highest level of charges assessed during the year.

Pension—In Europe, a guest or boarding house.

Petit Dejeuner—Continental breakfast.

Piston Aircraft—A plane powered by an ordinary internal combustion (piston) engine(s).

Pitch—(1) The fore-and-aft motion of a ship at sea. (see Roll) (2) The longitudinal space occupied by an airline seat. If an aircraft is configured with a 28 inch seating pitch, there is 28 inches between the back of one seat and the back of the seat behind it.

Plant (Tourist, Travel or Visitor)—All facilities at a destination city, region or country.

Point-to-Point—Covering basic transportation only. A point-to-point fare is the basic rate from one city to another; a point-to-point sale covers only the cost of the ticket.

Porterage—Baggage handling service. The client on a tour which includes porterage should neither have to carry his luggage nor pay the man who does. Enlightened self-interest, however, might lead him to offer an occasional nominal tip.

Positioning—The movement of any air, land or sea vehicle for the purpose of placing it where it can perform a revenue service. A positioning cruise transports revenue passengers primarily to move a ship to another cruising ground.

Post-Convention Tour—An extension designed to offer a conventioneer a visit to an area more conveniently located to the convention site than his home as a supplement to his return trip.

Prepaid Ticket Advice—Notification (usually by teletype) from a carrier or agent in one city requesting a carrier in another city to issue prepaid transportation to a specified individual.

Pre-Registration—Room assignment and the filling out of registration cards prior to a guest's arrival. Often used for convention, meeting and tour guests.

Principal—The dominant participant in any given situation. More specifically in travel: (1) a primary producer of any unit of travel merchandise—an airline, a hotel, a shipline; (2) any person (or company) who assumes responsibility for a travel program; anyone who pays a commission to another for selling a travel program.

Prix Fixe—The price at which a specified table d'hote meal is offered.

Profile System, or Frequent Traveler File—A list, usually stored in a reservation system computer, of frequent travelers and very important customers, with information on their travel preferences, typical methods of payment and other information that is useful when making most bookings. With major reservation systems, each time one of these clients books a trip, profile information can be retrieved and transferred intact to the PNR, saving the time re-entering that information. Profiles can be used to store other kinds of more or less static information as well.

Promotional Fare—Any tariff below regular levels established to stimulate traffic, particularly at times when the carrier is not busy. Promotional fares are almost always roundtrips and are always restricted in one way or another. They may be good only at certain hours, or on certain days or in certain seasons. They may be good within certain time limits. As a general rule, the cheaper the fare, the more numerous the restrictions.

Proof of Citizenship—Any document that establishes the nationality of a traveler to the satisfaction of a government or carrier. If travelers are told to provide proof of citizenship, the implication is that some documentation of lesser stature than a passport will suffice. When in doubt, however, ask.

Proportional Fare—(see Arbitrary)

Protected—As in "commissions protected" "agents protected" or "all departures protected": A guarantee by a supplier or wholesaler to pay commissions, plus full refunds to clients, on prepaid, confirmed bookings regardless of subsequent cancellation of, for example, a tour or a cruise. (see Guaranteed Tour)

Provisioned Charter—The rental of a yacht without crew but with fuel and provisions for a voyage. (see Bareboat Charter)

Pseudo-PNR—Commonly used phrase to describe any reservation or other information stored in an airline reservation system using the same format as a standard PNR (passenger name record). It's called pseudo because it does not include an air reservation. It can show details of any kind of sale: car rental, hotel, package tour, cruise or even travel insurance.

PTA—(see Prepaid Ticket Advice)

PTM—(see Passenger Traffic Manager)

Public Charter—A charter form adopted by the CAB in 1978 which has no restrictions on price, length of stay, land arrangements or advance booking. One-way flights and discount prices are permitted at the tour operator's discretion, so long as each charter group consists of at least 20 seats. Bonding and escrow provisions similar to those imposed on previous charter types are required for the protection of passenger funds. Not all foreign governments have accepted these liberal rules.

Pullman—(see Railroad Classes of Service)

Q

Queue System—A computerized tickler file consisting of as many as a hundred queues provided as part of an automated reservation system. The system vendor assigns tasks to some of the queues, and such tasks include providing information on agency clients who are waitlisted, informing agents of bookings affected by fare or schedule changes, reminding counselors to print tickets on certain days, for example. Agents can decide how to use other queues to store information for reference purposes.

R

Rack Rate—The official tariff as established and posted by a principal, however, not usually used by tour operators.

Receiving Agent—(See Reception Operator)

Receiving Airline—A carrier which will begin transporting a passenger after his arrival at an interline point.

Reception Agency—(see Reception Operator)

Reception Operator—A tour operator or travel agent who specializes in services for incoming visitors.

Reconfirmation—A statement of intent to use a reservation. Under some airline rules reserved space may be resold unless the passenger reconfirms within specified time limits.

Red Book—Official Registry (and directory) of American Hotel & Motel Association.

Regional Airline Association—A trade group representing commuter airlines.

Registry—A ship's certificate indicating ownership and the national flag under which she sails. Registry, however, is non-indicative of the quality of a ship or the nationality of her officers, crew or service personnel.

193

Regulatory Agency—A local, state, federal or international organization with authority to approve or disapprove the actions of carriers and/or their conferences.

Rep—A representative, either an individual or a company, empowered to act for a principal, usually in a sales or reservation capacity. (see Airline Rep, Hotel Rep)

Res (or Rez) Agent—A person who takes reservations and/or sells tickets, usually for an airline.

Reservationist—A carrier (usually airline) employee who accepts, verifies and confirms reservations (often by telephone) but does not actually write tickets.

Responsibility Clause—That section of a brochure that spells out the conditions under which a tour is sold. It should include the name(s) of the company or companies who are financially responsible.

Retail Agency—The business establishment of a retailer; a subdivision of a wholesale and retail travel organization.

Return—British and European designation for round trip, as a return ticket or return rate.

Revalidation Sticker—An attachment to a flight coupon confirming that a change has been made to an original reservation.

Revenue Aircraft Mile—One airplane operated one mile in a commercial service.

Revenue Passenger Mile—One paying passenger carried one mile, a basic statistical unit in the airline industry.

Roll—Side to side motion, as of a ship at sea.

Roundtrip Fare—The rate charged for a trip to a destination and return by the same route to the point of embarkation.

RPM—(see Revenue Passenger Mile)

RSM—Regional Sales Manager.

Run of the House Rate—A flat price at which a hotel agrees to offer any of its rooms to a group.

S

SABRE—American Airlines' reservations system.

Salon—(see Parlor)

Sample—A room, such as a studio or parlor, in which merchandise will be displayed.

Sandwich War—A promotional contest involving meal service on North Atlantic IATA airlines. The rules in 1957 stated that meal service in Economy Class could consist of sandwiches. SAS kicked off the battle by publishing a picture of a lavish array of open-faced sandwiches. U.S. carriers protested that such smorgasbords had not been envisioned when the rule was made.

SATO—(see South American Tourism Organization)

SATW—Society of American Travel Writers.

Scheduled Airline—An airline operating over one or more routes pursuant to published schedules.

Scheduled Airline Ticket Office—A joint office at a U.S. military establishment operated jointly by carriers. Formerly known as a JAMTO or Joint Airline Military Ticket Office.

Second Class Hotel—(see Hotel Classifications)

Segment—In an air itinerary: a leg or group of legs from boarding to deplaning point on a given flight.

Self Drive—Refers to an automobile that may be rented without a driver.

Sell/Sell—A message used by a host airline when confirming a seat on an off-line carrier. Sell/Sell tells the agent who is using the host line's automated reservation system that there is space available on the off-line carrier's flight. This advice is based on the inventory that the off-line carrier has made available to the first, or host, carrier. The host line later informs the second carrier of the seat sale without asking for a specific confirmation.

Service Charge—(1) A specified percentage of a hotel bill (usually 10% or 15%) assessed against a guest; in return the guest presumably is relieved of the responsibility for tipping. (2) A fee charged to a client by a travel agent in addition to the commissions paid to him by his principals.

Service Compris—Inclusive service at a restaurant. Generally the bill contains an extra 10-15% to pay for the service. Therefore tipping is not expected except, perhaps, for some small change.

Shells—(see Tour Shells)

Shoulder Fare, Rate or Season—On some air routes, and at a few hotels a price level between that charged during the low season and the high season. In the Caribbean, however, rates during the shoulder seasons (spring and fall) have at times been at the year's lowest level.

Shuttle—Type of air service operated in the U.S. by Eastern Airlines and in Great Britain by British Airways under which any passenger showing up before a scheduled departure is guaranteed a seat even if a second jet has to be operated with only one passenger. Eastern Airlines' high-frequency service operates every hour on the hour. Offered in the U.S. between New York and Boston and New York and Washington; in the U.K. between London and Glasgow, London and Edinburgh, London and Belfast.

Sidetrip—(see Extension)

Single—Any facility or reservation to be used by one person.

Single Carrier Reservation System—A computerized reservation package that is provided by one airline and gives the agency subscriber direct access to that carrier's computer. However, agents can use one carrier's computer to book space on most other airlines as well as many other travel products, including hotel rooms and car rentals.

Single Entity Charter—An air charter sponsored and paid for by a single person, company or organization. None of the passengers may be charged for any of the travel involved.

Single Supplement—An extra charge assessed to a tour purchased for single accommodations.

SITCA—Secretaria de Integracion Turistica Centro Americana, a promotional organization of Central American national tourist offices.

Skal—Corruption of Skoal, a toast, "to your health."

Skal Club—(1) A local social organization of the travel industry. (2) the International Federation of Skal Clubs, the worldwide organization of local Skal clubs.

Sleeper—A railroad car with sleeping accommodations.

Sleeperette—A modified first class seat used on some airlines which reclines to an almost horizontal plane.

SNAVB—Syndicat National des Agences et Bureaux de Voyages (French Association of Travel Agents).

SNCF—(see Societe Nationale des Chemins de fer Francais)

Societe Nationale des Chemins de fer Francais—The name used in France for the French National Railroads.

Sonic Boom—A loud explosive sound caused by the shock wave preceding an aircraft traveling at supersonic speeds.

Space—Reservation(s), or the capacity, generally in terms of seats on common carriers or of rooms in hotels or inns, to accept reservations.

SPACE—Selected Professional Agents Coordinating Enterprises, Inc., a consortium of retail travel agents.

Space Available—(see Available)

Special Interest Tour—A tour designed to appeal to clients with a curiosity or a concern about a specific subject. Most such tours provide an expert tour leader and usually visit places and/or events of special interest to the participants.

Special Service Request—A request to an airline that is providing transportation for a specific service requested by the customer, such as a kosher meal, a wheelchair or a special seat assignment. The request (dubbed SSR) is stored in the passenger name record maintained by the airline's computer.

Split Charter—(1) An aircraft (motorcoach or ship) which has been engaged to perform a specific flight by two or more distinct legal entities. (2) That portion (40 or 60 seats, for example) of an aircraft engaged for a specific flight or flights.

SRV—Schweizerisches Reiseburo Verband. (Swiss Federation of Travel Agents)

SS—Steamship

SST—(see Supersonic Transport)

Stabilizer—a device designed to eliminate or dampen a ship's tendency to roll. A gyro-stabilizer constantly adjusts the attitude of underwater vanes at the command of a gyroscope. A flume stabilizer employs the weight and motion of water introduced to and expelled from tanks in a rhythm counter to the ship's roll. Stabilizers do not affect a ship's pitch. (see Bow Thruster)

Standard Sleeping Car—Canadian designation for old-fashioned Pullman sleeping car.

Standard Ticket and Area Bank Settlement Plan—A system established by ATC under which travel agents report and remit airline ticket sales to various banking institutions established as area banks. In addition to the domestic airlines, most foreign air carriers which do business in the U.S. and Canada handle their agency accounts through the plan.

Standard Ticket Stock—(see ticket stock)

Standby—A passenger on a waitlist. He may actually appear at an air terminal prepared to travel in the event of a cancellation or a no-show; in that circumstance he may be called a go-show.

Standby Fare—A promotional tariff based on a conditional reservation. The holder of a standby ticket is not eligible to board his flight until all passengers who have or want confirmed reservations have been accommodated.

Star, One (Two, Three, Four or Five)—A hotel rating. (see Hotel Classification)

Stateroom—A sleeping room on a ship; may imply more luxury than a cabin.

Steamship—Virtually any large, ocean-going vessel. There are few true steam vessels (ships powered by steam engines or steam turbines) in active service today, but shipping men still consider themselves to be in the steamship business.

196

Stern—The rear end of a vessel.

STOL—Short takeoff and landing, usually referring to an aircraft with such capabilities.

Stopover—The act of leaving (or right to leave) a flight for an indefinite period (usually 24 hours or more). Virtually all regular fares offer unlimited stopovers at scheduled route stops. Promotional fares, however, often include stopover surcharges, limit the number allowed or forbid them altogether.

Strand—To abandon passengers during or just prior to a prepaid travel program, for example at an air terminal where passengers have gathered prior to departure. Most strandings have been caused by the business failure of tour operators, a few by failures of carriers.

Stripped Package—(1) A package that includes the bare minimum of ingredients necessary to qualify it for an IT number. (2) Any package or tour offering inferior accommodations and/or omitting some or many of the features usually included in an inclusive tour.

Student Card—(see International Student Identity Card)

Studio—A hotel room with a couch or couches that convert into beds. Thus, a studio may be used as a parlor or a bedroom.

Subcontractor—A local operator which provides service for a wholesaler.

Summer Fare, rate or season—On many air routes and at many destinations, either the highest, lowest or middle level charged during the year. On the North Atlantic, summer air fares are at peak; in the Caribbean, summer air fares and hotel rates are lower than those for winter but may be higher than those for spring and fall.

Supersonic Transport—An aircraft capable of operating at a speed exceeding that of sound.

Supplement—(1) An extra, or better grade of, service. (2) A charge for same. (see Single Supplement)

Supplemental (or Supplemental Airline or Carrier)—An airline certificated to offer passenger and cargo charter services. Sometimes called a charter airline or a non-sked.

Supplier—The actual producer of a unit of travel merchandise; a carrier, hotel, sightseeing operator, etc.

Supporting Documents—Additional papers necessary to verify a transaction; driver's license, birth certificate, health card, visa and passport are examples.

T

Table d'Hote—A full-course meal served at a fixed price; may or may not offer alternatives.

Tariff—(1) Any individual fare or rate quoted by any supplier. (2) Any class of fares or rates, for example, a youth tariff. (3) Any published list of fares or rates established by any supplier. (4) A published compendium of listed fares or rates for any category of supplier. (5) An official publication containing all fares or rates, conditions of service, etc.; a legal tariff.

TC1, TC2, TC3—(see Traffic Conferences)

Technical Stop—An en route stop, either planned or unplanned, for refueling, crew changes or other operational needs, but not for discharging passengers or taking on new revenue traffic. Also called a nontraffic stop.

TES—Turbine Electric Ship.

Theme Park—(1) A large, regional amusement facility with rides, shows, restaurants, shops and other attractions and often having its own security, food service, laundry, maintenance and medical facilities and staffs. Architecture, decoration, uniforms, music and other means suggest a theme or image for the entire park or for designated sections of it. Sometimes the term "major theme park" is used to make a distinction between such facilities and (2) Small amusement parks, relying solely on local clientele, using various means to suggest a theme.

The Travel Research Association—A professional society of travel industry market research specialists.

Third Level Carrier—Air-Taxi or commuter airline not regulated by the CAB, but by the FAA.

TIAC—(see Travel Industry Association of Canada)

Ticket—The written or printed evidence that an individual (or group of individuals) is entitled to transportation, entry, etc. Airlines: The passenger ticket and baggage checks, including all flight, passenger and other coupons therein, issued by the carrier, which provide for the carriage of the passenger and his baggage.

Ticket Agent—A carrier employee who takes reservations and sells tickets. The federal government uses this term to describe anyone who sells an airline ticket including travel agents and tour operators.

Ticket Stock—Ticket blanks held by carrier employees and travel agents to be filled out and validated at which point they become tickets. Standard Ticket Stock may be used on any U.S. airline that is a member of ATA and on many foreign IATA carriers. Some carriers print their own ticket stock.

Tonnage—Measures of a ship's size. Dead-weight tonnage: the number of tons of cargo, fuel, stores, etc. a ship can carry. Displacement tonnage: the number of tons of water she displaces; her actual weight. Gross tonnage: a measurement used to express the volume of enclosed space on a ship; the measurement used in giving the size of passenger vessels; one gross register ton equals 100 cubic feet of enclosed space. Net registered tonnage: gross tonnage minus the space occupied by crew quarters, engines, fuel, stores, etc.

TOSG—(see Tour Operators Study Group)

Tour—Any prearranged (but not necessarily prepaid) journey to one or more places and back to the point of origin.

Tour Basing Fare—A reduced-rate excursion fare available only to those who buy prepaid tours or packages. Inclusive tour, group inclusive tour, incentive group, contract bulk inclusive tour, tour basing, and group roundtrip inclusive tour basing fares are all tour basing fares. Any fare offered by a carrier on which a travel agent may claim a higher commission if he sells specified ground arrangements at the same time. (see Airline Classes of Service)

Tour Brochure—(see Brochure)

Tour Departure—Related to the operation of any published tour: the date of the start by any individual or group of a particular travel program; by extension, the entire operation of that single tour. For example: a tour operator may schedule a European escorted group tour with 16 departures, that is, the same basic tour may be operated 16 times.

Tourism—The business of providing and marketing services and facilities for pleasure travelers. Thus, the concept of tourism is of direct concern to governments, carriers, and the lodging, restaurant and entertainment industries and of indirect concern to virtually every industry and business in the world.

198

Tourist Card—A document issued to prospective tourists as a prerequisite for entry and departure. A tourist card is usually the only travel document required by the issuing country, i.e. no passport is required, but a passport without the card is insufficient.

Tourist Class—In general, accommodations or establishments somewhat below top grade. Shiplines: Segregated, less than first class service. Airlines: Unofficial designation for economy or coach service. (see Airline Classes of Service)

Tourist Hotel—(see Hotel Classifications)

Tour Leader—Strictly speaking, a person with special qualifications to conduct a particular travel group, i.e. a botanist who conducts a garden tour. Often, however, used inaccurately to designate a courier.

Tour Manager—A courier, especially one employed to conduct a prepaid tour from beginning to end, including any transocean legs.

Tour Operator—A company which creates and/or markets inclusive tours and/or performs tour services and/or subcontracts their performance. Most tour operators sell through travel agents and directly to clients. (see Contractor, Operator and Wholesaler)

Tour Operators Study Group—A trade association of British tour operators.

Tour Organizer—An individual, sometimes a travel agent, who organizes a group of passengers to participate in a special, prepaid tour. An organizer does not necessarily have conference appointments, nor does he usually pay commissions.

Tour Package—(see Package)

Tour Shells—Brochures containing artwork, graphics and/or illustrations but bare of copy, which are to be overprinted by tour operators or wholesalers.

Tour Wholesaler—(see Wholesaler)

TPPC—(see Transpacific Passenger Conference)

Track—Charter route, particularly the route followed by a series of back-to-back charters.

Traffic Conferences—Within IATA, the sub-organizations of carriers that serve the three areas into which IATA has divided the world (see Areas One, Two and Three). Thus TC1 sets rates and makes rules applicable to Area One, TC2 for Area Two, etc.

Transatlantic Passenger Shipping Conference—The chief North American executives of the now dissolved Atlantic Passenger Shipping Conference members. (see International Passenger Ship Association)

Transfer—Local transportation and porterage as from one carrier terminal to another, from a terminal to a hotel or from a hotel to a theater. The conditions of a tour contract should specify whether transfers are by private car or motorcoach and whether escort service is provided.

Transpacific Passenger Conference—The promotional and regulatory association of shipping companies which offer passenger services in the Pacific.

Transport Workers Union of America—An AFL-CIO trade union representing many categories of U.S. airline employees but not pilots. The TWU also has affiliates in the railroad, missile and transit industries.

Travel Agent Magazine—A twice-weekly U.S. trade publication.

Travel Industry Association of America—A non-profit association of companies and government organizations formed to promote travel to and within the United States.

Travel Industry Association of Canada—A trade association embracing the entire range of Canadian travel and transportation and related industries and governmental organizations.

Travelnews—A British trade newspaper.

Travel South, U.S.A.—A non-profit regional travel promotional organization formed by the governors of eleven Southeast states.

Travel Trade Gazette—A British trade newspaper.

Travel Trade Magazine—A U.S. weekly trade publication.

Travel Weekly—A Ziff-Davis trade newspaper published twice each week and read by the vast majority of U.S. and Canadian travel agents.

TS—Turbine Electric Ship.

TSS—Turbine Steamship.

TTG—(see Travel Trade Gazette)

TTRA—(see The Travel Research Association)

Turbofan Jet—Aircraft powered by a turbojet engine(s), the thrust of which has been increased by the addition of a low-pressure compressor (fan).

Turbojet—Aircraft powered by an engine(s) incorporating a turbine driven air compressor to take in and compress air for fuel combustion, the combustion gases and/or heated air being used both to rotate the turbine and create a thrust-producing jet.

Turboprop—An aircraft powered by an engine(s) in which the main propulsive force is supplied by a gas turbine which drives a propeller.

Twin—Room for two guests with two single beds.

Twin Double—Room for two, three or four people with two double beds.

TWU—(see Transport Workers Union of America)

U, V

UATP—(see Universal Air Travel Plan)

U-Drive—(see Self Drive)

UFTAA—(see Universal Federation of Travel Agents Associations)

United States Tour Operators Association—A nationwide organization of tour operators.

United States Travel & Tourism Administration—The official U.S. Commerce Department agency for the promotion of tourism.

Universal Air Travel Plan—The credit card system originally organized by the U.S. domestic airlines but now recognized by all IATA airlines.

Universal Federation of Travel Agents Associations—A world organization of national travel agents trade associations.

UPAV—Union Professionelle des Agences de Voyages Beige (Belgian Association of Travel Agents).

Upgrade—To move to a better accommodation or class of service.

Uplift Ratio—A formula whereby some governments limit the charter activity of foreign airlines by requiring their outbound charter operations to be balanced by a certain ratio of incoming traffic.

Upper—A berth on a ship or train that is above another.

U.S.A. Rail Pass—A pass good for rail travel in the U.S., sold for a flat rate for a specified number of days. It can be purchased in the U.S. and is available for sale in foreign countries.

USTOA—(see United States Tour Operators' Association)

USTTA—(see United States Travel & Tourism Administration)

Video Display Terminal—A generalized term to describe any of a variety of TV-like display screens that allow the user of a computer to see what is being entered into the computer and to read the information the computer is sending out. The terminals are frequently used with airline reservation systems and back-office automated accounting systems in travel agencies.

Validation—Imprinting a piece of airline ticket stock with the special stamp that makes it a legal ticket.

Validator—(1) A mechanical device used in validation. (2) Any of the special airline die plates used in such a device to imprint tickets.

Verification—(see Documentation and Proof of Citizenship)

Visa—An official authorization appended to a passport permitting travel to and within a particular country or region.

Visible Horizon—At sea, the distance from the vantage point of an observer to the horizon. The distance can be figured roughly by this formula: The horizon-distance (in miles) equals the square root of the height of an observer's eye from the water (in feet). Thus, at 49 feet the visible horizon is seven miles away. On a typical promenade deck, eye-level will be 64 feet above water; the horizon will be eight miles away and the upper-works of a large ship will be visible on a very clear day at a distance of up to 17 or 18 miles.

Visit USA Fares—Air tariffs offering visitors to the U.S. reduced fares on domestic travel.

Volume Incentive—(see Override)

Vouchers, Tour—Documents issued by tour operators to be exchanged for accommodations, meals, sightseeing and other services. Sometimes called coupons.

W, Y

WACTI—(see Western America Convention & Tourist Institute)

WAD—(see World Aviation Directory)

Wagon Lits—The international company which operates sleeping cars on European railroads.

Waitlist—A list established by a supplier, particularly an airline, of customers who seek space on a date or a time that is sold out.

Warsaw Convention—The original agreement under which international (and many domestic) airlines established the principle that their legal liability for passengers and cargo should be limited. The original Warsaw passenger limitation was $8,333. That figure was raised to $16,666 by the so-called Hague Protocol. At present, most major airlines have signed the 1968 Montreal agreement raising the per-passenger limitation to $75,000 and waiving the right of defense.

Weigh Anchor—To raise the anchor of a ship.

Western American Convention and Tourist Institute—Composed of state, city, and private organizations in the travel and convention industry; promotes travel to 13 Western states.

Wet Lease—The rental of a vehicle, particularly an aircraft, with crew. A pure wet aircraft lease would include full operational and cabin crew, supplies, fuel and maintenance services. Most lease contracts fall somewhere between outright wet and bone dry. (see Dry Lease)

WHO—(see World Health Organization)

Wholesaler—A company that usually creates and certainly markets inclusive tours and FITs for sale through travel agents. Often used interchangeably with tour operator, but several distinctions might be drawn: (1) A wholesaler presumably sells nothing at retail; a tour operator often does both. (2) A wholesaler does not always create his own products; a tour operator virtually always does. (3) A wholesaler is less inclined than a tour operator to perform local services. Industry reportage often fails to make distinctions, and, to confound things further, many travel companies perform any or all of the functions of travel agent, contractor, tour operator and wholesaler.

Winter Fare or Rate—Either the most expensive or the least expensive level depending on the area under discussion. On the North Atlantic, air fares are lowest in winter; in the Caribbean, both air fares and hotel rates are highest in winter.

World Aviation Directory (including World Space Directory)—A Ziff-Davis world reference, covering 135 nations, of the personnel and equipment of all known airlines, the personnel and products of aerospace manufacturers and distributors, and the personnel and interests of publications, organizations and government agencies.

World Bank—Mutual welfare organization established to aid national governments; its personnel is international.

World Health Organization—A specialized United Nations agency that provides technical public health assistance at the request of governments. WHO constantly surveys the ebb and flow of communicable diseases throughout the world, advising governments on establishing and enforcing requirements for various vaccinations as a prerequisite to travel between specific areas. The certificates of vaccination recorded on travelers' World Health cards enable governments to erect barriers to halt the spread of disease and at the same time permit foreign visitors to enter and depart as they wish.

World Service Authority—Private organization which promotes interests of invalid travelers. Also issues "citizen of the world" passports, mostly for stateless refugees or for businessmen with worldwide interests who prefer not to be identified with a particular country.

World Tourism Organization—Formerly the International Union of Official Travel Organizations, now a United Nations affiliated organization of government tourist offices.

World Travel Directory—A Ziff-Davis annual worldwide reference for domestic and international travel planners. Includes pertinent data on the sales personnel and outlets of travel agents and tour operators; air, sea and rail carriers, car rental and sightseeing firms; Consulates, embassies and national and state tourist offices; travel and hotel representatives; publications, schools and associations; and motel/hotel systems.

WTD—(see World Travel Directory)

WTO—(see World Tourist Organization)

Yacht Broker—A dealer in used pleasure boats; many yacht brokers act as agents for pleasure boat charters.

Youth Hostel—(see Hostel)

INDEX

G

H

I

K

L

M

N

O

P

R

"Rack" rate, 61
Railroads, 23
Rail travel, 23
Resorts, 71, 103
Revnes, Richard, 115, 121
Royal Cruise Lines, 115

S

Sacramento First National Bank, 122
Self-contained groups, 13-14
Seminars, 65-66, 71, 103
Sheraton, 30
Ship companies, 30
Shuttle buses, 26
Sightseeing, 26, 32
Simmons Market Research, 109
Sorensen, Lynne, 123
Steamship companies, 30
Stephan, Bill, 128
Super-Saver fare, 36

T

Tax-deductible expenses, 87
TGV, 24
Time leverage, 113-114
Tours, 26, 67, 83
Tour conductor, 58-61
Tour leader, 58-61
Tourism, 36-39
Trade schools, 15, 55
Trailways, 25
Trans-Pacific Passenger Conference (T.P.P.C.), 36
Transportation, 23-29, 32, 33, 73
Travel agents, 24, 25, 27, 30, 34-36, 43, 49, 61, 64, 65, 83, 85, 88, 89, 95, 103, 104, 121, 122
Travel agency/agencies, 7, 8, 11, 13, 14, 23, 28, 29, 32, 33, 34-36, 42, 43, 44, 46, 49, 52-55, 58, 59, 61, 62, 64, 65, 74, 80, 83-86, 87, 89, 95, 101, 106, 114, 115, 123, 127

Travel agency owners/managers, 11-15, 79, 81, 85
TravelAge West, 67, 71, 79
Travel and Tourism Government Affairs Council, 114
Travel and Tourism Press, 108
Travel Consultant, 5-6, 7-8, 9, 10, 13, 14, 28, 29, 31, 34, 41-55, 58, 59, 61, 62, 73, 74, 77, 78, 80, 83, 85, 86, 87, 88, 89, 95, 96, 101, 104, 107, 108, 109, 122, 123, 124, 127
Travel Counselor, 11
Travel industry, 6, 13, 23, 65, 73, 77, 114, 124
Travel parties, 101-103

U

United Airlines, 95
Universities, 15
U.S. Steel, 122

V

Volume bonuses, 35

W

Wholesale tour operator, 23, 32-34, 35, 58, 65, 89
Wholesalers, 29, 33

IMPORTANT INFORMATION FOR EVERY READER

FRIENDS OF PRIMA

Would you like to meet the authors of books you read? Would you enjoy it if they were available to meet your friends, your club members, or your colleagues, with you acting as the host? Prima Publishing and Communications is launching a brand new program in book publishing. Called "Friends of Prima," this program is designed to develop close ties between authors and their readers. Here is how the program works.

Often, when a book is published, its author goes on a national tour to promote the new publication. These kinds of tours usually involve radio and television appearances, newspaper interviews, and autograph-signing sessions in local bookstores. When a Prima author goes on such a tour, he or she will also be available, *on a selective basis*, for autograph-signing parties in homes and for organizations. If you are interested in organizing an autograph-signing party and are willing to ensure the attendance of at least 50–100 people, we would like to hear from you.

Another excellent way to take advantage of the autograph-signing-party concept is to organize a fund raiser. If your club or non-profit organization decides to take advantage of this unique way to raise funds, part of the proceeds from the sale of the autographed books could be turned over to your organization.

Friends of Prima will also be notified of other special events as they occur in their area. If you would like to find out more about this special program, simply check the appropriate box on the attached post card and mail it to:

Ms. Nancy Martinelli, Director of Customer Relations
Prima Publishing and Communications
P.O. Box 1550
Carmichael, CA 95608

Or call Nancy Martinelli at (916) 972-8777.

MATERIALS AVAILABLE FROM PRIMA PUBLISHING AND COMMUNICATIONS

People who invest in themselves become more successful than those who don't. The average person asks, "How much does it cost?" The success-minded individual asks, "What is it worth?"

As a service to you, our reader, we have compiled a list of books that we believe you will find helpful in launching your new business career. Some of the choices are obvious in that they are travel related. Others have been chosen because they will help you develop the proper skills and attitude for business success. For your convenience, we have also compiled a special "starter pack" at a substantial discount to you. You can order without risk, since items purchased *directly* from Prima carry a full money-back guarantee when returned with the original invoice.

To order, simply fill out the attached card and enclose in an envelope with your payment or credit card information (Visa and MasterCard only). Or, for fast service on credit card orders, call Nancy Martinelli at (916) 972-8777. The minimum order must be at least $10.00. Please add $2.00 for postage, shipping, and handling. California residents add 6% sales tax.

CONFESSIONS OF A TOUR LEADER — Baxter and Corinne Geeting -U.S. $8.95

This is one of the best-written books of its kind. Recalling many years of leading tours throughout the world, the Geetings, a college faculty couple who took up tour escorting in order to enjoy worldwide travel, spin an hilarious tale of their adventures and mishaps. Between fits of laughter, you will learn much about the art of tour escorting. *Confessions* is a winner of the National Writers Award for 1982.

AN INSIDER'S GUIDE TO THE TRAVEL GAME — John Baldwin Seales - U.S. $7.95

This is an excellent introduction to the "ins and outs" of traveling. Written from the traveler's point of view, *The Travel Game* contains valuable insight for anyone in the travel business. The chapter on travel tips alone is worth many times the price of the book.

THE WAY TO GO — Elaine Lerner with C.B. Abbott -U.S. $6.95

Although subtitled *A Woman's Guide to Careers in Travel*, *The Way to Go* is an excellent reference for both men and women who would like an overview of the career opportunities available in travel. Elaine Lerner is an ex-housewife who, starting a small travel business in her own home, now operates her own multi-million dollar retail/ wholesale travel agency.

TOLL-FREE PHONE BOOK — U.S. $9.95

This is a gold mine of useful travel information. Included are toll-free numbers for:
- Travel and tourist information services
- Travel and tour agencies
- Cruises and special-interest vacations
- Reservation services
- Hotels, motels, and other accommodations
- Airlines
- Car rental and leasing agencies
- Other transportation services
- And much, much more

THE MAGIC OF THINKING BIG — David J. Schwartz - U.S. $3.95

This classic by the well-known psychologist will help any budding Travel Consultant develop a winning attitude. Successful people think BIG—you can learn how.

★ GETTING STARTED PACK ★

Order all five of these terrific books to help you get your travel career off and running. Retail value: U.S. $37.75 Special price: $32.75 (a $5.00 discount)

Quantity	Book Title	Price	Amount
	Travel Free! How to Start and Succeed in Your Own Travel Consultant Business	$19.95	
	Confessions of a Tour Leader	$ 8.95	
	An Insider's Guide to the Travel Game	$ 7.95	
	The Way to Go	$ 6.95	
	Toll-Free Phone Book	$ 9.95	
	The Magic of Thinking Big	$ 3.95	
	"Getting Started Pack" (A $5.00 Savings)	$32.75	

Make checks payable to:
Prima Publishing & Communications

Please enclose this card along with your remittance in a separate envelope.

☐ I would like to pay by

Visa / MasterCard *(circle one)*

Card #: _____

Expiration date: _____

Signature: _____

Telephone #: _____

Sub Total: $ _____

CA residents add 6% tax: $ _____

Shipping and Handling: $ $2.00

Total: $ _____

Quantity	Book Title	Price	Amount
	Travel Free! How to Start and Succeed in Your Own Travel Consultant Business	$19.95	
	Confessions of a Tour Leader	$ 8.95	
	An Insider's Guide to the Travel Game	$ 7.95	
	The Way to Go	$ 6.95	
	Toll-Free Phone Book	$ 9.95	
	The Magic of Thinking Big	$ 3.95	
	"Getting Started Pack" (A $5.00 Savings)	$32.75	

Make checks payable to:
Prima Publishing & Communications

Please enclose this card along with your remittance in a separate envelope.

☐ I would like to pay by

Visa / MasterCard *(circle one)*

Card #: _____

Expiration date: _____

Signature: _____

Telephone #: _____

Sub Total: $ _____

CA residents add 6% tax: $ _____

Shipping and Handling: $ $2.00

Total: $ _____

From: (Please print clearly)

_____

_____

_____
                     (Zip)

Stamp

Check as many boxes as are appropriate:

To:
    Prima Publishing and Communications
    Post Office Box 1550
    Carmichael, CA 95608

☐ I would like to be on your mailing list.

☐ I am interested in being notified of special events in my area.

☐ I am interested in hosting an Author's Autograph Party. My telephone number is ( ) _____.

☐ I am placing a book order. (See back of card.) When ordering books, enclose this card in envelope and mail with remittance.

From: (Please print clearly)

_____

_____

_____
                     (Zip)

Stamp

Check as many boxes as are appropriate:

To:
    Prima Publishing and Communications
    Post Office Box 1550
    Carmichael, CA 95608

☐ I would like to be on your mailing list.

☐ I am interested in being notified of special events in my area.

☐ I am interested in hosting an Author's Autograph Party. My telephone number is ( ) _____.

☐ I am placing a book order. (See back of card.) When ordering books, enclose this card in envelope and mail with remittance.

IN RESPONSE TO YOUR INQUIRIES...

• Ben and Nancy Dominitz are accomplished and popular speakers in seminars, workshops, and conventions on the subject of success in sales and developing a productive and realistic self image. They are available for speaking on a limited basis.

• As a service to travel agents, Cal Co Am, Inc., a marketing corporation, has set up a consulting arm headed by Ben Dominitz to help travel agencies successfully implement profitable and ongoing outside sales marketing programs. Consultation is available either in person or by telephone.

• Quantity discounts of *TRAVEL FREE!* are available to travel agencies, travel and trade schools, and other volume purchasers.

Please address all inquiries to:

Ms. Nancy Martinelli, Director of Customer Relations
Prima Publishing and Communications
Post Office Box 1550
Carmichael, CA 95608
or call:
(916) 972-8777

*Share the
Good News!
Tell a Friend
about*
Travel Free

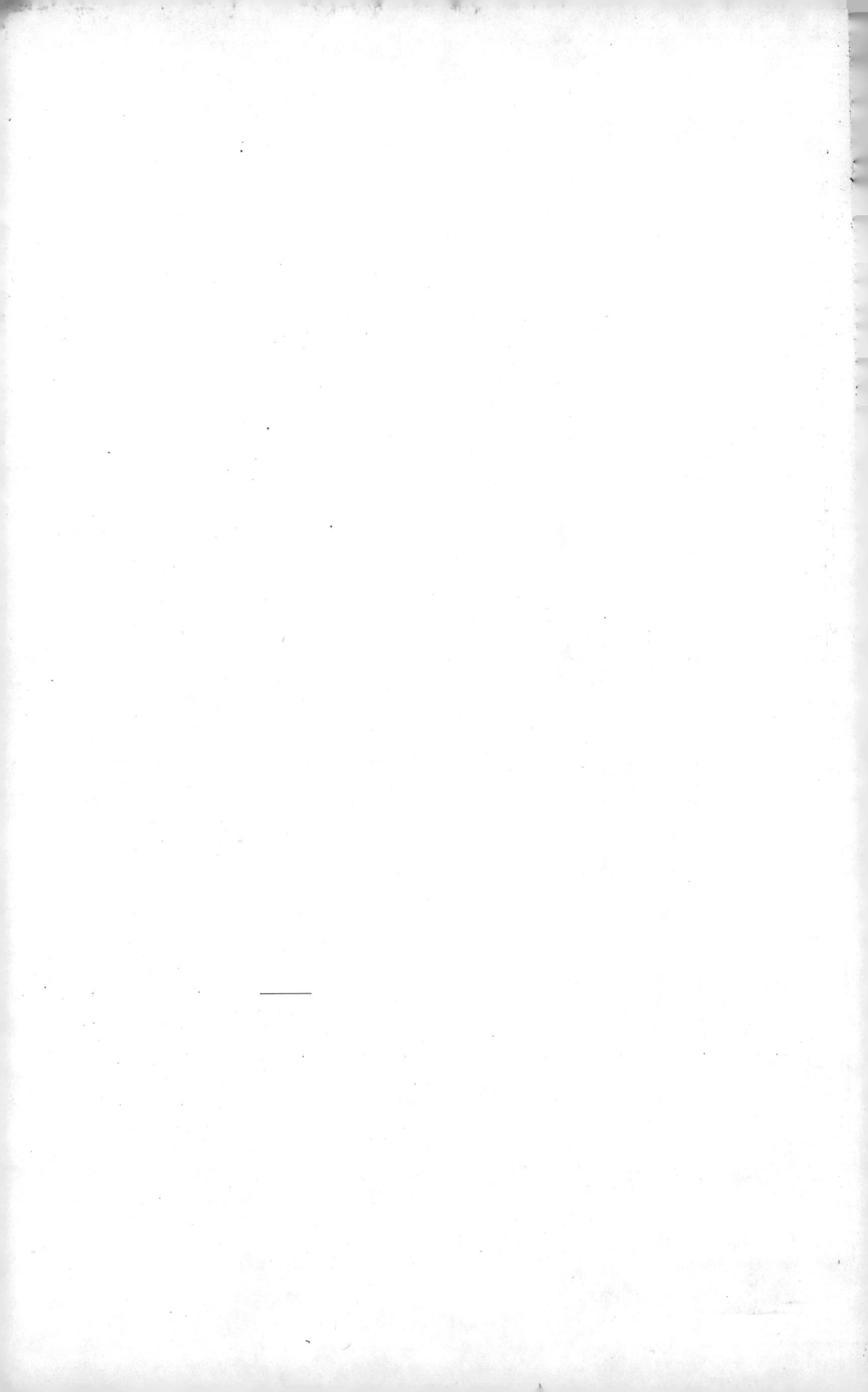